# Asian Art

Volume v, Number 1 Winter 1992
Published by Oxford University Press
in association with the Arthur M. Sackler Gallery, Smithsonian Institution

## MESOPOTAMIAN ART IN THE LOUVRE

# The Louvre's Collections of Early Mesopotamian Art

*Françoise Tallon*

The Mesopotamian antiquities of the third millennium B.C. are principally from three sites where French excavations took place: Tello, in southern Mesopotamia, to which is owed the discovery of the Sumerians; Mari, capital of a kingdom on the Middle Euphrates; and Susa, in southwestern Iran. These sites have yielded artifacts representative of the three great divisions of the third millennium: the Early Dynastic period (ca. 2900–2350 B.C.), when the land of Sumer was divided into rival city-states, political units centered on and controlled by a single city; the era of the first Mesopotamian empire, ruled by the kings of Agade from 2350 to 2190 B.C.; and the Neo-Sumerian period, or "Sumerian renaissance," from about 2190 to 2000 B.C. (fig. 1).

## The Excavations at Tello

Tello, site of the ancient city of Girsu, is located halfway between Baghdad and the Persian Gulf, between the Tigris and Euphrates rivers, 418 miles northwest of Basra and 11 miles from a branch of the Tigris, the Shatt el Hai. Tello was occupied during the Ubaid period, around 4000 B.C. Its best-known and most brilliant eras were those of two powerful dynasties, separated by the intermediary of the Akkadian empire. The first dynasty, founded by the king Ur-Nanshe around 2475 B.C., reigned over Lagash, one of the city-states of Sumer in the Early Dynastic period. The second dynasty gave the state a particular renown at the time of the Sumerian renaissance, especially during the reigns of Ur-Bau and his son-in-law Gudea, around 2130 B.C. The city retained its importance under the Third Dynasty of Ur (2112–2004 B.C.), then declined at the beginning of the second millennium and disappeared during the seventeenth century. In the second century B.C., an Aramaean prince, Adad-nadin-ahhe, installed himself there and built a palace that his successors used until the second century A.D.

Tello consists of a great oval site measuring 2.5 by 1.9 miles, composed of a number of secondary mounds, or tells, which the excavators designated by letters. In the north, on Tell A, was the palace of the Aramaean prince

built on the site of the Eninnu, the temple dedicated two millennia earlier by Ur-Bau and Gudea to Ningirsu, the tutelary divinity of Lagash. At the time of the Sumerian renaissance this site was the heart of an immense sanctuary, a veritable holy city surrounded by ramparts. In the Early Dynastic period the religious center of the city was located farther south, on Tell K, where remains of the Eninnu sanctuary dating to this early period were recovered.

It was on this site that Ernest de Sarzec (1837–1901), the French consular agent posted at Basra, undertook excavations in 1877 following

the discovery of statues under circumstances that have never been completely clarified (fig. 2). With great determination, he succeeded in carrying out eleven campaigns of excavations between 1877 and 1900. These excavations were complicated by the oppressive climate, difficult relations with the Ottoman Turkish administration, and insecurity in that frontier province of the Ottoman empire, which was occupied by more or less unsubdued Arab tribes.

Actual work began in 1880 and 1881. Backed by the French Ministry of Foreign Affairs, Sarzec obtained permission from the Ottoman sultan to excavate throughout ancient Chaldea (southern Babylonia) and to take finds away. He began with excavations of Tell A, where he had previously discovered fragments of a colossal statue of Gudea. There he found eight other diorite statues of this prince and one of Ur-Bau, as well as a large bald head. The other large head, known as the Head with a Turban, came from Tell H, located farther to the south.

On May 31, 1888, Sarzec returned to Paris with these extraordinary finds, including the beautiful statue of the Woman with a Scarf, two more modest statues representing wives of Gudea, and foundation figurines,

sculptured vases, bronzes, tablets, inscribed bricks and cones, votive weapons, jewelry, and baked clay figurines. In addition to these Neo-Sumerian objects were several works of the mid-third millennium B.C. from an exploration made on Tell K.

The arrival of this collection in Paris did not pass unnoticed. The minister of public instruction secured an allocation from the legislature permitting the Louvre to acquire it. The Department of Oriental Antiquities was created to receive the collection and entrusted its management to a well-known scholar of ancient Greece, Léon Heuzey (1831–1922). Most noteworthy was that a number

Figure 2. Ernest de Sarzec, seated in the center, with his team at Tello, ca. 1878

of the objects were inscribed in an unknown language—Sumerian—whose existence had been postulated by the Assyriologist Jules Oppert (1825–1905). The arrival in France of these inscriptions was to permit their decipherment and to elaborate the culture of a people until then known only by name.

A new regulation governing antiquities, instituted by the Ottoman administration in 1884, later interrupted the excavations at Tello for seven years, during which time the site was seriously pillaged. With the intervention of the count of Montebello, the French ambassador at Constantinople, Sarzec was able to resume his work in 1888 and 1889. During these years he explored Tell K, which yielded a number of objects of the greatest importance for the Early Dynastic period. Despite a law forbidding the export of excavated finds, diplomatic negotiations permitted the Louvre to obtain, among other objects, fragments of the famous Stela of the Vultures, two reliefs of Ur-Nanshe, and the macehead of Mesalim, a Sumerian king in the Early Dynastic period.

Excavations that followed discovered, among others, thousands of tablets on Tell V. When Sarzec died in 1901, the monuments essential to the knowledge of the Sumerians were already known. The three archaeologists who succeeded him at the site brought to light interesting related information. In the course of four campaigns between 1903 and 1909, Gaston Cros (died 1915) continued excavations on Tells A, K, and V, and opened new areas. He discovered on Tell B important fragments of the stelae of Gudea.

After World War I, the concession for the excavation, together with a share of the finds, was given to France by the newly established country of Iraq. Between 1929 and 1931, the abbot Henri de Genouillac (1881–1940) resumed work in several of the areas of excavation inaugurated by his predecessors. On the slopes of Tell V he identified the remains of the temple of Gudea's personal god Ningishzida and that of Ningishzida's wife, Geshtinanna, unfortunately robbed of their contents in 1924. Finally, from 1931 to 1933 André Parrot (1901–1980) pursued the investigation of the prehistoric levels. He discovered the residential quarters dating to the end of the third millennium and the beginning of the second millennium and brought to light a large, enigmatic building. Parrot left the site in 1933 to investigate the newly discovered site of Mari, and his departure marked the end of the excavations at Tello.

## The Excavations at Mari

In August 1933, a group of Bedouin tribes discovered on the site of Tell Hariri an inscribed bust representing a divinity. Following the discovery, René Dussaud (1868–1958), a curator in the Department of Oriental Antiquities at the Louvre, obtained the concession for excavations under the auspices of the National Museums and entrusted the directorship of the project to André Parrot.

Work began in December 1933, and Parrot quickly discovered in a trench opened at the western edge of the site a number of statues dedicated to Ishtar, the goddess of war, including one inscribed by the official Ebih-il (see "Art and the Ruler," fig. 16). On January 23, 1934, the excavators found a statue of Lamgi-Mari, king of Mari, whose inscription demonstrated that the site was the ancient city of Mari, which according to the Sumerian King List was the seat of the tenth dynasty following the Flood. The King List is an ancient composition giving the names of the kings of Sumer with the lengths of their reigns from mythological times "before the Flood" to about 2000 B.C.

Tell Hariri is a large, relatively low mound, measuring about 3,960 feet by 3,960 feet and located on the right bank of the Euphrates about one and one-half miles from the river. The remains preserved today represent only a part of the ancient city, which has been undermined over the course of the centuries by a canal that flowed to the northeast. Apparently founded at the beginning of the third millennium, Mari covered a vast area from its inception, but its early history is still poorly known. Chance has dictated that two great periods have been brought to light by the excavations: the second half of the Early Dynastic period, from about 2600 to 2350 B.C., and the period of the Amorite dynasties, dating to the beginning of the second millennium. This period is known by a palace measuring nearly seven and one-half acres, where thousands of tablets of major importance for the history of the ancient Near East have been discovered. The defeat of the king of Mari, Zimri-Lim, by Hammurabi of Babylon (reigned 1792–1750 B.C.) around 1760 B.C.,

led to the pillage and destruction of the site. Between these two brilliant eras, the period of the Akkadian empire and that of the princes known as the *shakkanaku* are less well known. After Hammurabi's conquest, Mari lost its importance, but existed until the Seleucid period (312–83 B.C.). Archaeologists have found only a few Middle and Neo-Assyrian and Neo-Babylonian tombs dating to these dark centuries.

Mari's prosperity was due to its location on the trade route between Mesopotamia and the Mediterranean or Anatolia. Raw materials—wood, stones, and metals—passed through Mari, transported by river and overland routes.

In the middle of the third millennium, the civilization of Mari was modeled on that of the land of Sumer but the majority of its population spoke a Semitic language, as indicated by the language used for inscriptions on statues. The excavations brought to light remains of a royal palace of this period, situated in the center of the city and surrounded by temples dedicated to various Sumerian and Semitic divinities. The temples contained numerous statues of worshipers, panels made of shell mosaic, and carved stone vases. The sculpture was strongly influenced by that of Mesopotamia but displayed local peculiarities, such as the bulbous headdress, or *polos,* worn by women.

André Parrot carried out twenty-one campaigns at Mari between 1933 and 1974. Until World War II, the finds were shared between Aleppo and the Louvre; following the war they were taken to the museum in Damascus. Consequently, the collections

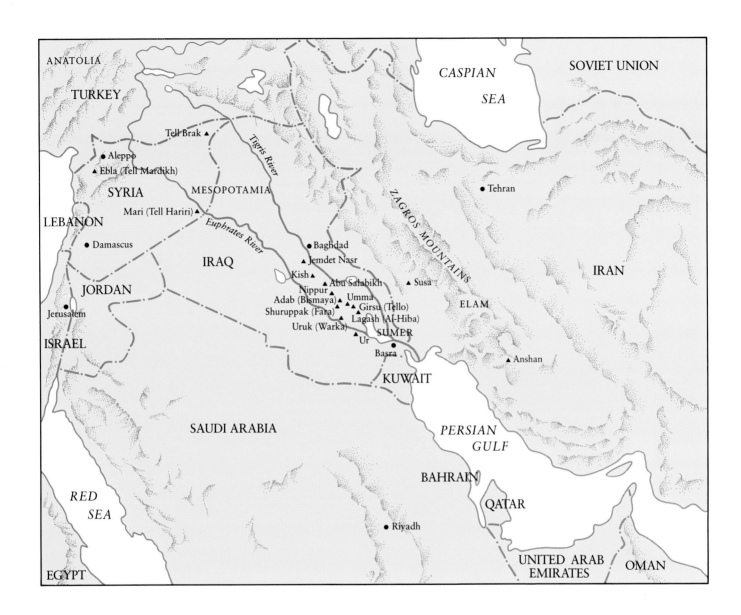

Mesopotamia and
Environs

▲ ancient city
  (followed by modern name)
● modern city

of the Louvre consist essentially of objects recovered in the temple of Ishtar and the Amorite palace before 1939.

Jean Margueron, a French archaeologist, resumed excavations at Mari in 1979. To define Mari's economic, social, and cultural role among the powers of the Bronze Age, Margueron opened a number of trenches so he could study the urban development of the site, its geographical and ecological environment, and the relations of the kingdom with its neighbors. His work is still in progress, and each successive season produces precious new finds.

## The Akkadian Antiquities at Susa

Since the capital of the Akkadian empire has not been found, the products of royal workshops that have survived to the present—victory stelae

Figure 3. The discovery of the stela of Naram-Sin, king of Agade ca. 2250 B.C., at the site of Susa, 1898. This monument is also illustrated in "The Birth of Writing," fig. 11.

and large-scale sculptures—have come almost exclusively from Susa, where they had been taken as booty in the twelfth century B.C., about a thousand years after they were made. In this period, Susa, an ancient city founded around 4000 B.C., was one of the capitals of Elam, a kingdom situated to the east of Mesopotamia. In 1158 B.C., the Elamite king Shutruk-Nahhunte led a devastating attack on Babylonia, then ruled by a Kassite dynasty, which his son would overthrow shortly thereafter.

The site of Susa was identified by W. K. Loftus (1821–1858), who explored it between 1850 and 1854. It was excavated between 1884 and 1886 by Marcel Dieulafoy (1844–1920), who was primarily interested in the Achaemenid palace built by Darius. In 1897, the newly established French mission to Persia began work under the direction of Jacques de Morgan (1857–1924) and discovered on the Acropolis, the religious center of the city, the victory stela of Naram-Sin, fourth king of the dynasty of Agade (fig. 3), and the obelisk of his father, Manishtusu. In the following years statues of these two kings were found, as well as victory stelae of Sargon, the founder of the empire.

The Mesopotamian collections of the Louvre have been assembled primarily as a result of excavations conducted by French missions in the Near East. For more than a century, however, curators in the Department of Oriental Antiquities have sought to expand them through the purchase or donation of acquisitions.

Françoise Tallon received her Ph.D. in Near Eastern archaeology in 1982 and has worked in the Department of Oriental Antiquities, Louvre, since 1967. She is the author of *Métallurgie susienne I: De la fondation de Suse au XVIIIe s. avant J.-C.* (Paris, 1987) and is currently writing a book on the reign of Gudea.

# The Birth of Writing in Ancient Mesopotamia

*Béatrice André-Salvini*

Note: All objects illustrated in this article are from the collections of the Louvre, Paris.

Figure 1. Statuette representing the priest-king, in ritual nudity, southern Iraq, ca. 3300 B.C. Limestone, 11¼ × 3¾ × 2½ in (29 × 9.4 × 6.3 cm)

Writing began around 3300 B.C., in the south of what would later be called the land of Sumer. The political, social, and cultural circumstances necessary for its invention came together in a period of profound change as people began to form urban communities.

The term *cuneiform writing* was given in the eighteenth century by its first investigators to the graphic system used most extensively in the ancient Near East. The signs of this system were composed of elements in the form of wedges (Latin, *cunei*). Although this form was only the final stage in this system's three-thousand-year evolution, the term *cuneiform* has traditionally been used for the entire system.

Writing cannot develop until a society is conscious of itself as a social unit, for the symbols must be known by everyone. There also must be a suitable medium for conveying them. These conditions were present very early in southern Mesopotamia. Village cultures, characterized by painted pottery styles, succeeded one another there from the beginning of the sixth millennium. Creatures, things, and symbols were represented by simple, condensed elements, and the systematic repetition and stylization of certain decorative motifs were established. Beginning in these remote periods, decorated pottery implies the discovery of clay as a useful material for representing and communicating thought. This material remained of fundamental significance throughout the early history of writing in Mesopotamia. The evolution of writing was based on the medium of clay.

When people in the valley of the Tigris and Euphrates rivers learned to control water by digging irrigation canals, new possibilities in agricultural production necessitated a new form of community organization. As a significant part of the population became engaged in crafts and in trade, professional specialization and social hierarchy became increasingly pronounced. The population grew and was concentrated in the important centers, which from this point on can be described as cities.

By 3300 B.C., Uruk (in the period of Level IVa) was a prosperous city that engaged in trade to obtain the materials and products it lacked. This commerce provided an impetus to the arts. Monumental architecture appeared, and the temple of the tutelary divinity was also a great administrative center under the authority of a chief who seems to have had both a religious and a political role and is traditionally called the "priest-king," or Sumerian EN[1] (fig. 1).

Relations among individuals became complex. The large group of people who worked for the temple had to be fed, and administrators had to manage their assignments and salaries as well as flocks and incoming and outgoing merchandise. As human memory is limited, a new and unified system of reference was sought to preserve oral communications. It was from these administrative and economic needs that writing was born. Writing was not an isolated invention in this period of great change and creativity. Indeed, several other important discoveries were made at the same time—the lost-wax method to facilitate the mass production of copper tools, for example, and the potter's wheel to improve and standardize the making of pottery.

The invention of writing was preceded by the invention of accounting and derives from it. Accounting transactions were first recorded with clay tokens. These small objects have been found at a number of sites in the Near East dating from the Neolithic period, beginning in the seventh millennium. They are in a variety of conventional forms—spheres, cones, cylinders, tetrahedrons—symbolizing the animals or commodities to be counted. Tokens of the same type exist in several scales corresponding to different orders of magnitude, such as units or

tens. Around 3400 B.C. at Uruk—as at Susa, in southwestern Iran—one would carry out a commercial transaction and verify a delivery according to the number and kinds of tokens in a spherical clay envelope known as a *bulla*. If there was a dispute, opening the *bulla* would settle it. One day someone had the idea of indicating the number of commodities on the surface of the clay *bulla* while it was still wet, either by impressing the tokens themselves on the surface or by making notches for each of them. The clay *bulla* was thus no longer needed; it was flattened and became a tablet. Then the accountants thought to add, next to the numbers, a drawing that symbolized the object or animal counted. The principle of writing was discovered.

## The First Writing

Uruk is regarded as the birthplace of writing, since it is there that the earliest evidence—in the form of thousands of small tablets of clay or stone—has been found. But two tablets, each bearing a number and a drawing of an animal, perhaps datable to the same period, have been found at Tell Brak in northern Mesopotamia in north Syria. This discovery suggests that the invention by the accountants and administrators of Uruk was not isolated. Slightly later, around 3000 B.C., the Proto-Elamite civilization created, on a neighboring model, a system of writing designed to express its language, Elamite. This writing, which has not yet been deciphered, did not develop further.

The first writing is extremely diffi-

Figure 2. Pictographic tablet, Jemdet Nasr, Iraq, ca. 3100 B.C. Clay, 1¾ × 1½ × ¾ in (4.6 × 4.1 × 2.1 cm). This accounting record is divided into columns. The holes represent the numbers 1 (conical notches) and 10 (circular impressions). The pictograms represent an ear of barley, a cow (schematized by the head), and the female symbol (the feminine genitals).

cult for us to decipher. Although the signs do not allow an identification of the language they transcribe, it is most likely Sumerian. The first tablets bear only the essentials of the message to be preserved: they are isolated words, not phrases. Incised in clay or sometimes in stone are figures meaning numbers and signs for persons, animals, objects, or commodities, repeated in a standardized way that for Sumerians recorded amounts and to us testifies to a repertory of signs widely recognized and accepted by this community. But, like an entry taken from an index whose title is lacking, the drawing of the head of a cow next to the figure representing 10 does not tell us what sort of transaction concerning these ten cows has been recorded.

These first signs were pictograms and logograms. *Pictograms* (picture-signs) are immediately identifiable drawings of objects or creatures; *logograms* (word-signs, also called *ideograms*) are signs expressing a word either for a concrete thing or an abstract idea. The method of writing was linear, with signs formed by straight lines and curves. Pictures were represented as they appear to the viewer, and the direction of reading was vertical, from top to bottom and from right to left. Some signs were representational; others were already stylized and simplified, indeed symbolic (fig. 2). To invent writing, the Sumerians transcribed into pictures the symbols of their society, symbols known to them but many of which are now lost to modern understanding. Some objects were represented abstractly even in the first attempts at writing. Such is the case with the animal most often counted— the sheep. The word was written by a cross in a circle representing the animal in its pen, perhaps a simple transcription of a clay token long in use. The principle by which the number of sheep were recorded is easy for us to understand since even today we use repeated strokes to record repeated objects quickly. But other, more elaborate symbols cannot be deciphered. We understand them only because they appear in later cuneiform whose meaning is well attested in more evolved texts.

## The System of Writing

Originating as a memory aid, writing became increasingly elaborate in the course of the following centuries.

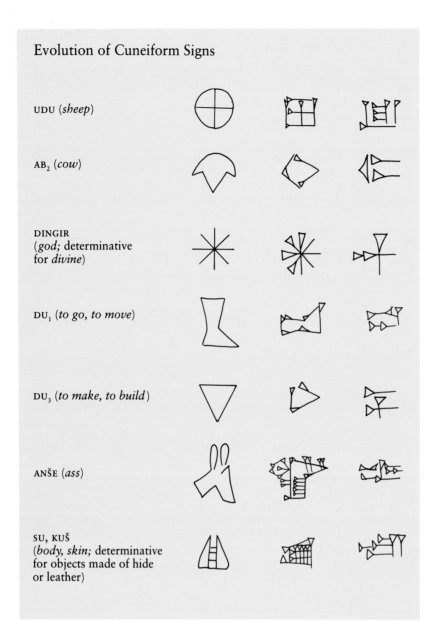

## Evolution of Cuneiform Signs

UDU (*sheep*)

AB₂ (*cow*)

DINGIR
(*god; determinative
for divine*)

DU₁ (*to go, to move*)

DU₃ (*to make, to build*)

ANŠE (*ass*)

SU, KUŠ
(*body, skin; determinative
for objects made of hide
or leather*)

Ways of writing signs evolved at the same time that the possibilities of representing the nuances of language expanded.

Pictographic, linear writing, incised with a pointed tool, changed rapidly, the signs soon losing all resemblance to primitive figural sketches (see Evolution of Cuneiform Signs). This phenomenon is due to the medium of clay, the only natural resource in this region deprived of stone and wood. Its limitations determined the shape of the signs—and thus the destiny of the writing hereafter called cuneiform. As it is difficult to sketch curved lines on wet clay, the signs were composed in straight lines, soon pressed and no longer incised, by means of a reed pen with a triangular end that produced impressions in the form of wedges. The basic element of this writing is the wedge, which could be horizontal, oblique, or vertical, the different combinations of which formed a sign.

As the system of writing evolved, the creation of signs formed by the combination of two distinct signs increased the amount of information that could be recorded and permitted greater precision (see Composite Ideograms). In addition, the same ideogram came to be understood not only in its first sense but also as a symbol of related things or actions in a process known as the polyphony of signs. Thus, the same sign was used to write *mouth* (KA), *nose* (KIR₄), and *word* (INIM) as well as the idea of speaking (DU₁₁) and crying (GU₃). The reader had to choose among these different meanings according to the context, and making the correct choice was not always easy.

To remedy this difficulty, scribes invented determinatives—classifications placed before or at the end of a word (and probably not pronounced aloud) that specified the category to which the word belonged: god, person (for proper names), star, bird, country, stone object, and so forth.

The need to transcribe proper names and the grammatical relation-

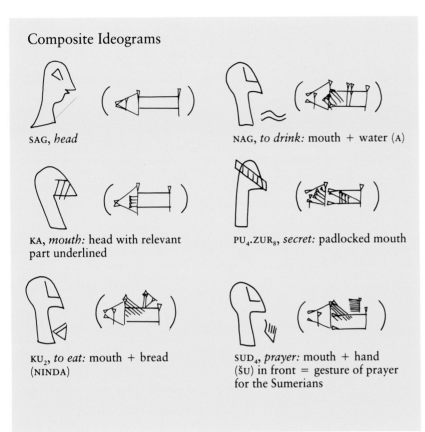

**Composite Ideograms**

SAG, *head*

KA, *mouth:* head with relevant part underlined

KU₂, *to eat:* mouth + bread (NINDA)

NAG, *to drink:* mouth + water (A)

PU₄.ZUR₈, *secret:* padlocked mouth

SUD₄, *prayer:* mouth + hand (šu) in front = gesture of prayer for the Sumerians

ships of whole phrases led to the development of phoneticism, whereby logograms represented not only a word but a sound. Thus, the sign for *mouth* (KA) served to express the sound "ka." This development was facilitated by the structure of Sumerian, an isolated language not related to any known language family and whose relationship to other languages is unknown. Its addition of fixed syllabic elements—prefixes, infixes, suffixes—to the principal word (root noun or verb) expresses grammatical relationships and is a function described as agglutination. For example, DU₃ means *to build;* MU.DU₃, *he builds;* MU.NA.DU₃, *he builds for him;* MU.NA.NI.DU₃, *he built it there for him.*

Sumerian's monosyllabic words imply numerous homophones—that is, words having the same sound but different meanings and thus written by different signs. Examples in English are *bear* and *bare* or *tail* and *tale.* In Sumerian, sixteen signs are pronounced "du." To transcribe and distinguish them one from another, modern decipherers have numbered them: DU₁ means *to go;* DU₃, *to make, to build;* and DU₆ *mound, tell.*[2] The ancients were able to distinguish these homophones through nuances of tone that were later noted by an arbitrary sign. DU₁, for example, is sometimes employed in the texts on building in place of DU₃ to mean *to build.* Use of these signs permitted an overall reduction in the repertory of signs from nine hundred in the early period to about five hundred around 2400 B.C. The development of a syllabic system permitted the writing of phrases showing relations among words and recording all the nuances of the spoken language, but the writing of Sumerian always remained primarily ideographic.

## The Development of Writing, 3000 B.C.–2200 B.C.

Around 3000 B.C., the transition to phoneticism was well under way, as the contents of texts testify. From the beginning the scribes of Uruk classified the words of their language and the signs of their writing for pedagogical purposes. These so-called lexical lists remained the basis for learning writing and languages throughout the history of cuneiform. In the period of Uruk IV, pictographic writing re-

Figure 3. Figure with Feathers, carved relief, Tello (ancient Girsu), southern Iraq, ca. 2700 B.C. Limestone, 7 × 5¾ × 1½ in (18 × 15 × 4 cm). This is one of the oldest inscribed reliefs known. A personage, who could be the priest-king, stands in front of the door of a temple represented by two reed poles. The inscription, divided into cases, covers all the space not used for the image. The inscribed signs are of very archaic form; the text may be a contract for the sale of a field.

corded lists of professions and like items such as metal objects and textiles. These repertories were systematized in the following period at Uruk (Level III) and at Jemdet Nasr,[3] located farther to the north, around 3000 B.C., along with the first diffusion of writing. Of some four thousand archaic texts recovered at Uruk to the present, about 450, or 15 percent, are lexical lists. Analysis now under way may supply the key to a number of archaic signs still undeciphered. The other tablets are economic archives of the great cultic and palatial complex of the Eanna at Uruk.

As writing progressed, the contents of texts grew richer, and it became increasingly possible to represent all the elements of the Sumerian language (fig. 3). In turn, this expansion of the possibilities of writing must have contributed to the evolution of the language.

In the Early Dynastic period (ca. 2900–2350 B.C.), the land of Sumer was divided into small city-states that fought among themselves for preeminence. Around 2600 B.C. at Abu Salabikh and at Shuruppak, the modern site of Fara, about 31 miles north of Uruk, literary tablets appeared alongside contracts and economic documents. These are the first written versions of Sumerian literature, preserving a tradition still largely oral. Often simple root words only suggest the narrative; the reader must supply the missing elements, and today that is sometimes impossible. Fluctuations in the notation of grammatical elements require that each phrase be contained in a case, the sentences clearly separated. Within a case, the signs appear in no clear order. But the tradition of lexical texts is, from this point on, well established, with very elaborate lists of domesticated and wild animals, birds, trees and objects made of wood, plants, textiles, geographical lists, as well as lists of mathematical and economic terms.

Around the middle of the third millennium, the direction of reading changed. Signs were moved one-quarter turn to the left, and henceforth tablets were read in lines and from left to right. This change resulted from practical reasons con-

Figure 4. Sumerian economic tablet concerning the yoking of asses to a plow (compare Evolution of Cuneiform Signs), Tello (ancient Girsu), southern Iraq, dated to Year 4 of the reign of Enentarzi, prince of Lagash, ca. 2360 B.C. Clay, 2¾ × 2¾ × 1 in (7.3 × 7.3 × 2.4 cm)

nected with the fact that writing on tablets was cursive. Split up, reversed, simplified, used for their sound and no longer for what they represented, the signs lost symbolic content but gained speed in evolution and in the flexibility to record languages other than Sumerian. The original symbolism was never altogether forgotten, however, and throughout Mesopotamian history to the end of cuneiform writing around the beginning of the first millennium A.D. the original ideogrammatic significance of the signs remained current.

In the middle of the third millennium, cuneiform writing began to spread outside the borders of the land of Sumer, to Mari on the Middle Euphrates. Slightly later, during the twenty-fourth century, it traveled as far as Ebla (modern Tell Mardikh, near Aleppo) in Syria, where, although the majority of texts were written in Sumerian, there also appeared a cuneiform recording of a local Semitic language.

The best-known phase of the Early Dynastic period is the final one, between 2500 and 2350 B.C. A significant part of the archives of the dynasty that reigned at that time in the state of Lagash is now in the collections of the Louvre. These are principally the economic archives of the temples, recovered during excavations at the site of Tello (fig. 4). The grammar by this time was well established, and phrases, still contained within cases, were written in normal word order and with all their grammatical elements.

In monumental inscriptions, however, the primitive way of reading—vertically and from right to left—survived until the beginning of the second millennium. Cursive writing, on clay, evolved rapidly and became dissociated from official writing on stone or metal, which appeared around 2600 B.C. These rare and precious media, imported from distant regions, were intended for commemorative inscriptions about great actions of the princes. Texts related to construction of temples, votive objects (fig. 5), and historical narratives were sometimes accompanied by figural representations.

Throughout Mesopotamian history, following a tradition that goes back to this early period, rulers undertook extensive building projects to

Figure 5. Votive relief of Ur-Nanshe, king of Lagash, Tello (ancient Girsu), southern Iraq, ca. 2495–2465 B.C. Limestone, 15½ × 18¼ × 5½ in (40 × 47 × 14 cm). Ur-Nanshe is shown as the king who builds, carrying a basket of bricks for the construction of the temple of the god Ningirsu. Opposite him, the king's wife and sons are identified by their names inscribed on their clothing. In the lower register, the king is present at a banquet commemorating the construction of the building. He is surrounded by four additional sons and his cupbearer, who stands behind him. The text tells us about the commercial relations that the princes of the Sumerian city-states maintained with distant lands: "Ur-Nanshe, the king of Lagash, the son of Gunidu . . . built the temple of Ningirsu. . . . The boats of Tilmun brought wood from that country [for the temple]." Tilmun is the island of Bahrain, which was the transit area for hard and precious stones and metals coming from the land of Meluhha (India) and the land of Magan (Oman).

achieve merit in the eyes of the gods and glory in the eyes of humankind. Royal texts, intended to last forever, were written on hard and precious materials. Most of them were foundation documents, made to be buried under doors or incorporated into the walls of buildings to commemorate their construction. Addressed to the gods or to future rulers who would restore the buildings—a frequent necessity in this land where walls were made of mud—the texts were reproduced in several similar examples or on different forms: stone boulders, mud bricks, stone tablets joined to copper figurines ending in a point, clay nails whose heads would extend above the walls in which they were

embedded, stone door sockets. The text bore the name of the divinity to whom the building—usually a temple—was dedicated, the name of the ruler, his lineage and titles, the purpose of the construction, sometimes an account of the circumstances that motivated it, and wishes for the long life of the dedicator.

Among these royal inscriptions are texts inscribed on objects offered to the gods by rulers or dignitaries (figs. 6, 7): the objects include maceheads, statues, stelae, stone or metal vases, reliefs, and texts that can be described as "historical," written on stone stelae (fig. 8), cones (fig. 9), and ceramic vases—a noble and durable use of clay. These documents describe events

Figure 6. Votive relief of Dudu, priest of the god Ningirsu at the time of Enmetena, prince of Lagash, Tello (ancient Girsu), southern Iraq, ca. 2425–2375 B.C. Bitumen, 9¾ × 8½ × 3 in (25 × 22 × 8 cm). The lion-headed eagle (symbol of Ningirsu) grasping two lions was the emblem of Lagash. The personage wearing the *kaunakes*, a skirt made from sheep's hide, has his name inscribed next to him: *Dudu*, written by the sign DU₁ (a foot), repeated twice and read phonetically.

of the time when the Sumerian city-states, governed by a hereditary king or prince, whose authority was derived from the great local god, attacked one another over boundary disputes or the domination of a neighboring city. The conflict between Lagash and its neighbor and rival Umma began over boundaries and shared irrigation canals. It was recounted on several documents of which the most famous is the Stela of the Vultures of the king Eanatum (reigned ca. 2450 B.C.) (see fig. 8). The text, written in cases in the spaces left undecorated by the sculptor, is illustrated by scenes in low relief on both faces of the stela. On one side is Ningirsu, the god of

Lagash, holding captives from Umma in a net; on the other side is Eanatum in a chariot leading his troops on foot. Originally the text must have included about 830 cases or phrases. Two generations later, Enmetena, grandson of Eanatum, recounted the vicissitudes of the conflict in his own era and traced them to their origins one hundred and fifty years earlier, when Mesalim, king of Kish, reigned over all the land of Sumer and served as arbitrator in the dispute (fig. 10). In what was truly the work of a historian, Enmetena explained that the people of Umma never observed the treaty of alliance defining the boundaries between the two city-states and that he settled the dispute by pleading before Enlil, the great god of Sumer, to establish his title and authority (see fig. 9).

Cuneiform writing developed above all through its adaptation to languages other than Sumerian. In the period of the first developments in writing, the Sumerians formed the numerical majority of the population, and their culture was unrivaled. Farther north, however, a Semitic-speaking population had existed for a long time; Semitic names are found in Sumerian texts of the Early Dynastic period. Around 2335 B.C. Sargon, cupbearer of the king of Kish, founded the first Mesopotamian empire—the empire of Agade, whose capital has not yet been located. Thus appeared the first texts written in a Semitic language—Akkadian.

Akkadian scribes used cuneiform signs to transcribe their language, the vocabulary and structure of which were completely different from Sumerian. In Akkadian, three conso-

Figure 7. Plaque in the form of a votive beard, dedicated by a queen of the Sumerian city of Umma, to Shara, the great god of Umma, southern Iraq, reign of Gishakidu, king of Umma, ca. 2370 B.C. Gold, 3¼ × 2½ × ¹⁄₁₂ in (8.5 × 6.7 × 0.2 cm). The plaque was probably intended to be attached to a statue.

nants in fixed order form the root of a word and define its general meaning. They operate with vowels that express the grammatical form of the word: thus *kšd*[4] means *to reach;* the infinitive is *kašadu(m),* while *ikšud* means *he reached.* In addition, Akkadian has a declension: nominative (subject), accusative (object), and genitive (relates to the noun).

Sumerian ideograms were taken as they were and simply read in the Akkadian language. For example, the sign designating a god, DINGIR in Sumerian, was pronounced "ilu" in Akkadian. But at the same time, the Sumerian pronunciation of signs was preserved and the writing system remained in large measure ideographic. To facilitate the understanding of texts, determinative ideograms for reading were generalized, and phonetic complements were introduced that indicated the last syllable of certain words written ideographically. This system allowed the reader to verify an interpretation. For example, GAN$_2$ is Sumerian for *field;* GAN$_2$-*lam* = *eqlam* is the accusative case in Akkadian.

The texts of the Akkadian period, in writing known as Old Akkadian, provide the first documentation in Mesopotamia of an organized empire.

Figure 8. Detail, Stela of the Vultures, victory stela, Tello (ancient Girsu), southern Iraq, reign of Eanatum, king of Lagash, ca. 2450–2425 B.C. Limestone, 6 × 4½ ft (1.80 × 1.30 m)

Figure 9. Inscribed cone of Enmetena (left), prince of Lagash, Tello (ancient Girsu), ca. 2425–2375 B.C. Terracotta, height 10½ in (27 cm), diameter of base 5 in (12.7 cm). The cone describes the history of settling the boundary dispute between the city-states of Lagash and Umma. At center and right are two inscribed cones of Urukagina, prince of Lagash, Tello (ancient Girsu), southern Iraq, ca. 2350 B.C.; terracotta, height 11 in (28.2 cm), diameter of base 6½ in (16.5 cm). The cones describe the social reforms instituted by this usurper prince to restore order in Lagash, which had been compromised by abuses of the rich and powerful.

Figure 10. Macehead dedicated by Mesalim, king of Kish, in the temple of Ningirsu at Lagash, Tello (ancient Girsu), southern Iraq, ca. 2550 B.C. Limestone, height 7½ in (19 cm), diameter 6¼ in (16 cm). The relief is decorated with the emblem of Lagash, the lion-headed eagle of Ningirsu grasping in his claws rearing lions, in a continuous frieze embracing the form of the object. Mesalim reigned over all the land of Sumer and was the arbiter in the dispute between Lagash and Umma.

In fact, the change from Sumerian to Akkadian took place in stages, with texts concerning authority, such as edicts and royal inscriptions, being the first to appear in the language of the ruling dynasty.

Clay tablets were by this time read in lines, from left to right, and no longer in cases, as the grammar had been established and written. Undoubtedly for convenience, however, since punctuation did not exist and out of a respect for tradition that was fundamental throughout Mesopotamian history, each phrase was contained in a line and each line separated from the others by a stroke made by the scribe. Documents discovered in frontier garrisons indicate that the diffusion of writing was due to military conquest as well as to expanding commercial networks.

The rulers of Agade extolled their glory in their inscriptions, but the literature of this period has not been recovered. The power and fame of the rulers are known principally by later copies of the texts or by subsequent literary texts. Sargon remained for posterity a mythical king. The history of his miraculous birth, his abandonment, and his discovery in a reed basket floating on the Tigris—like the later biblical Moses—as well as his assumption of power and his victories, and misfortunes were known even in Egypt. The conquests of his son, Naram-Sin, and Naram-Sin's impiety toward the gods, which according to his successors caused the downfall of the empire, were also part of the legend.

The accession of the dynasty coincided with a new idea that art should serve imperial ambitions and glorify the person of the king (fig. 11). Writing reflected this tendency toward the monumental. In inscriptions on stone—statues, stelae, votive objects, cylinder seals, foundation inscriptions—as well as on clay tablets, writing became sculpture and reached a formal perfection (figs. 12, 13, and 14; see also Royal Titulary of the Kings of Agade).

Figure 11. Victory stela of Naram-Sin, fourth king of the dynasty of Agade, ca. 2250 B.C. Sandstone, 6½ × 3½ ft (2.0 × 1.05 m). The king, at the head of his troops, scales a forested mountain in the Zagros Mountains, trampling the conquered foreigners. The stela was originally placed in the city of Sippar, Iraq, and was taken by a conquering Elamite king to Susa, southwestern Iran, where it was recovered in modern times.

Figure 12. Obelisk of Manish-tusu, third king of Agade, ca. 2260 B.C. Diorite, 54½ × 23½ × 23½ in (1.40 m × 60 cm × 60 cm). The monument bears 1519 cases of writing of great decorative elegance, following the ideal of the official art of the dynasty. The text records important purchases of land made by the king in the region of Kish. He carved them into four great domains, which he divided into lots to give them to his officers on whom depended the stability of the kingdom and whose loyalty he thereby ensured. The obelisk was originally from the region of Kish, Iraq, but found at Susa, southwestern Iran, where it had been taken as booty.

## Royal Titulary of the Kings of Agade

LUGAL KIŠ, King of Kish—a reference to the ancient hegemony of Kish over all the land of Sumer and cradle of the dynasty of Agade (see fig. 14). This prestigious title meant, therefore, "King of the Totality/Whole," that is, "King of the World."

## The "Sumerian Renaissance"

After the fall of the Akkadian empire, around 2190 B.C., the Sumerians regained power in a period that was the "swan song" of their culture. Around 2120 B.C. Gudea, prince of Lagash, dedicated to the god Ningirsu and to the principal divinities of the pantheon of his religious city Girsu (the modern site of Tello) the longest inscriptions in Sumerian that have come down to us. They were written on two large clay cylinders and on some twenty statues we know of him, in a rich and poetic language for which cuneiform could by this time render nuances. It is very difficult for the modern reader to grasp the original meaning and beauty of these texts. Sumerian can be deciphered, thanks to the lexical texts establishing lists of words classified by categories of objects or by analogies. Akkadian scribes and the Babylonians and Assyrians who succeeded the Sumerians

Figure 13. Cylinder seal and impression, of a scribe of Sharkalisharri, fifth king of Agade, dedicated for the deified king by a high official. Iraq, ca. 2200 B.C. Serpentine, height 1½ in (4 cm), diameter 1 in (2.6 cm). Engraved in the monumental style unique to Akkadian art, the inscribed cartouche is supported by two buffalo given water by nude heroes, acolytes of Ea, god of the waters, whose emblem—the flowing vase—they carry. Below, a river winds between two ranges of mountains indicated by the conventional scale pattern.

established bilingual Sumerian-Akkadian dictionaries, taking care even to record pronunciation. Their work has permitted us to understand for the most part this language that disappeared from memory until its rediscovery a hundred years ago. But some literary texts remain obscure.

Around 2112 B.C., the king Ur-Nammu founded the Third Dynasty of Ur, also called Ur III, for which considerable administrative documentation exists. During this period poets, writers, and scholars of "the house of tablets" (E₂.DUB.BA)—the

school and repository of literature—rethought, wrote down, and circulated the great literary works of the old oral tradition. These include hymns to the gods and to deified kings, myths, prayers, epics, philosophical essays, and wisdom literature. Writing had become a perfect and indispensable tool for the transmission of thought. But this great century of arts and letters—the "Sumerian renaissance"—was above all an attempt to restore a tradition on the edge of extinction. Around 2000 B.C., Ur, the capital, was de-

Figure 14. Vase inscribed "Rimush, King of Kish," second king of Agade, Tello (ancient Girsu), southern Iraq, ca. 2270 B.C. Alabaster, 6 in (15.4 cm), diameter 3¼ in (8.6 cm)

stroyed. Sumerian disappeared as a spoken language, replaced by Akkadian, which subsequently divided into two dialects—Assyrian in the north and Babylonian in the south. But Sumerian remained the language of learned culture to the end of cuneiform writing.

## The Diffusion of Cuneiform

It was at this time that cuneiform writing began to radiate throughout the Near East. Hundreds of thousands of documents were written in this complicated system, not only in the Sumerian language and then in Akkadian but also in the many other languages of different structure and families that it served to transcribe. These included Indo-European,

Semitic, and languages called Asianic, which lack affiliation with the two other language families. In the course of its long history, cuneiform writing penetrated the region extending from Egypt to Iran and from Anatolia to the island of Bahrain. In the middle of the second millennium, Akkadian in its Babylonian form served as the language of diplomacy; thus the great king of the Hittites and the pharaoh of Egypt could communicate in almost perfect Akkadian with the princes of the eastern Mediterranean coast. In the course of the first millennium, the political equilibrium was disrupted. Aramaean nomads entered Mesopotamia and introduced their language, which, written by means of a linear alphabet and involving few signs, was easy to learn and use. Cuneiform writing slowly regressed, but Akkadian, and even Sumerian, continued to be written in the religious and scholarly circles of Uruk and Babylon, which preserved the cuneiform tradition until the Christian era.

## Notes

1. Although it is usual to transcribe Sumerian terms in lower case Roman script, I have written them here in capital letters for clarity. Akkadian words are normally transcribed in italicized Roman script.

2. DU$_1$ can also be transcribed DU, DU$_2$ as DÚ, DU$_3$ as DÙ. In this system, the use of subscripts begins with DU$_4$. For consistency, I have used subscripts for DU$_1$–DU$_3$. The system is the same for all homophones.

3. Jemdet Nasr is the modern name of the site. When the written documents found through excavations at a site do not provide the ancient name, it is customarily known by its modern name. This is also the case with Abu Salabikh. Uruk, however, is the ancient name of the site whose modern name is Warka.

4. š is pronounced "sh."

## Further Reading

Amiet, Pierre. "La naissance de l'écriture ou la vraie révolution." *Revue Biblique* 97, no. 4 (October 1990): 525–41.

André, Béatrice, and Christiane Ziegler. *Naissance de l'écriture: Cunéiformes et hiéroglyphes.* Paris: Réunion des Musées Nationaux, 1982.

Catalogue of an exhibition held in Paris at the National Galleries of the Grand Palais, spring 1982, explaining the birth of writing in the Near East, the functioning of the cuneiform and hieroglyphic writing systems, the contents of texts, the profession of the scribe and his education, and the decipherment of cuneiform and hieroglyphs. Numerous illustrations.

André-Salvini, Béatrice. *L'écriture cunéiforme.* Paris: Editions de la Réunion des Musées Nationaux, Petits Guides du Louvre, 1991.

An introduction to cuneiform, illustrated with objects in the collections of the Louvre.

Bottéro, Jean. "L'écriture et la formation de l'intelligence en Mésopotamie ancienne." *Débat,* no. 62 (1990): 38–60.

———. *Mésopotamie: L'écriture, la raison et les dieux.* Paris: Gallimard, 1987.

A magisterial synthesis on the history and written civilization of ancient Mesopotamia.

Cooper, Jerrold S. "Cuneiform." *International Encyclopedia of Communications,* 1:438–43. New York: Oxford University Press, 1989.

Kramer, Samuel Noah. *The Sumerians.* Chicago: University of Chicago Press, 1963.

A synthesis of Sumerian civilization, including history, religion, literature, the Sumerian school, and the legacy of Sumer by a great Sumerologist who sought to make this austere discipline accessible to the general public.

Nissen, Hans. "The Archaic Texts from Ur." *World Archaeology* 17, no. 3 (1986): 317–34.

———. Peter Damerow, and Robert Englund. *Frühe Schrift und Techniken der Wirtschaftsverwaltung im alten Vorderen Orient.* Berlin: Franzbecker Verlag, 1990.

Catalogue of an exhibition of archaic tablets held in Berlin at the Museum for Pre- and Early History, Charlottenburg Palace, in spring 1990. The authors present current thinking on deciphering the archaic texts from Uruk.

Schmandt-Besserat, Denise. "Accounting in the Prehistoric Middle East." *Archaeomaterials* 4, no. 1 (Winter 1990): 15–23.

———. "The Earliest Precursor of Writing." *Scientific American* 238, no. 6 (June 1978): 50–59.

These two articles discuss the accounting techniques used before the invention of writing (tokens, *bullae,* and numerical tablets).

Walker, C.B.F. *Cuneiform.* Reading the Past series. London: British Museum Publications, 1987.

Béatrice André-Salvini is curator of tablets and inscriptions in the Department of Oriental Antiquities at the Louvre. She is coauthor with Christiane Ziegler of *Naissance de l'écriture: Cunéiformes et hiéroglyphes* (Paris: Réunion des Musées Nationaux, 1982) and author of numerous articles on the early history of writing and development of cuneiform in the ancient Near East.

Note: Louvre accession numbers: Figure (1) AO 5719; (2) AO 8856; (3) AO 221; (4) AO 13300; (5) AO 2344; (6) AO 2354; (7) AO 19225; (8) AO 2347; (9) AO 3004, AO 3149, AO 3278; (10) AO 2349; (11) Sb 4; (12) Sb 20; (13) AO 22303; (14) AO 3282.

# Art and the Ruler: Gudea of Lagash

*Françoise Tallon*

Note: Unless otherwise specified, all objects illustrated in this article are from the collections of the Louvre, Paris.

Figure 1. Head of Gudea, prince of Lagash, Tello (ancient Girsu), southern Iraq, ca. 2120 B.C. Diorite (greenstone), 9¾ × 9¾ in (25.2 × 25 cm)

Little is known about the historical background of Gudea, the Mesopotamian prince who has left us the greatest collection of statues and the longest texts we have in the Sumerian language (fig. 1). We do not know the exact dates of his reign, the extent of his territory, or the importance of his military expeditions. It is only through the religious hymns he addressed to the gods and through the products of the sculptural workshops he patronized that we can glimpse what, in his time, represented the idea of kingship.[1]

Around 2190 B.C., Mesopotamia entered a time of troubles that lasted for nearly a century. It began with the arrival of barbarian conquerers, the Guti, who brought an end to the empire of Agade and plundered its cities. Around 2120 B.C., a king of the city of Uruk, Utu-hegal, expelled the last of the Guti and restored the unity of the land of Sumer. His reign only lasted a few years since, in 2112 B.C., the governor of Ur, Ur-Nammu, rebelled against him and made Ur the capital of a new empire. Thus was initiated the Third Dynasty of Ur, which ended with the third millennium.

Toward the end of the era of foreign domination, a prince of Lagash named Ur-Bau (fig. 2) founded a new dynasty, inaugurating what is often called the "Sumerian renaissance." This term is only partly accurate, for although Sumerian again became the written language, the population of lower Mesopotamia still included a significant proportion of people speaking the Semitic language Akkadian. The heritage of the empire of Agade is also evident in the art and civilization of this era.

The Second Dynasty of Lagash was short lived, numbering only six princes: the founder; his three sons-in-law Ur-Gar, Nammahni (certainly a contemporary of Ur-Nammu), and Gudea (whose lineage is unknown); and the son and the grandson of Gudea, Ur-Ningirsu and Pirigme. We do not know the dates of Ur-Bau, the order of succession of his sons-in-law, or the length of each reign. We can only establish approximate reign dates by the year names customarily designated by the rulers, and not even all of these are known to us.

Scholars have traditionally placed Gudea in the period of the Guti in-

Figure 2. Statue of Ur-Bau, prince of Lagash, Tello (ancient Girsu), southern Iraq, ca. 2130 B.C. Diorite (greenstone), 26½ × 12¾ in (68 × 33 cm)

vaders, around 2150 B.C. A recent study, however, suggests that his reign, which lasted at least eleven years, was partly contemporary with that of Ur-Nammu of Ur.[2] Gudea's son, Ur-Ningirsu (fig. 3), then possibly his grandson, Pirigme, succeeded him, with reigns estimated respectively at four years and one year. Everything seems to suggest that Gu-

dea was not a vassal of the king of Ur and that the short reign of Nammahni was the last of the dynasty. The extent of the territory of Lagash under Gudea is also uncertain. It was centered around three main cities: Lagash, the original capital (today al-Hiba); Girsu (today Tello), the religious center and probably the residence of the prince; and Nina (today Shurgul). Gudea apparently controlled a part of southern Mesopotamia and access to the Persian Gulf. Indeed, dedications in his name have been recovered from Ur, Badtibira, Adab, Uruk, and Larsa; offerings he made in the north, at Nippur, seem to indicate that this region was not hostile to him. In any event, he brought from distant lands the materials necessary for his pious building projects. The stone diorite came from Magan (today Oman and perhaps also the opposite shore of the Strait of Hormuz). Lapis lazuli, carnelian, gold, and copper also came by way of the gulf. Other commodities were imported from the north and the northwest, like the cedar that came from the Amanus Mountains. These exchanges seem to have been essentially peaceful and could have taken place shortly after the eviction of the Guti, as suggested by a phrase in one of Gudea's texts: "Ningirsu [the god of Lagash], his dear king, opened to him the route from the Upper Sea [the Mediterranean] to the Lower Sea [the Persian Gulf]" (Statue B, VI, 64–49). Gudea only once mentions a military expedition, which took place in Elam against the city of Anshan, located in the modern Iranian province of Fars.

Gudea seems to have been an independent ruler, and the image of kingship strongly influenced by religion

Figure 3. Statue of Ur-Ningirsu, prince of Lagash, Tello (ancient Girsu), southern Iraq, ca. 2110 B.C. Alabaster, 21½ × 6¾ in (55 × 17 cm). Body: Louvre, Paris; head: The Metropolitan Museum of Art, Rogers Fund, 1947

that he has left can be considered as perfectly royal according to the criteria of the period. Indeed, the Sumerians had close ties with their gods, who were said to be responsible for the prosperity of the state and the well-being of the citizens. The ruler, who bore the title of *lugal* (king) or *ensi* (prince, governor) was believed to have been chosen by the gods to serve as an intermediary between them and humankind. This role of the king was fundamental, and his tasks were well defined. A hymn dedicated to Shulgi, the second king of the Third Dynasty of Ur, records that the king was born "to fill the granaries of the land with grain, to fill the storehouses of the land with all kinds of goods, to provide the trapper and the fisherman with birds and fish, to fill the stalls with milk and cream, . . . to administer justice in the land, to put an end to oppression."[3] This hymn summarizes what human and divine society expected of the king: to defend his territory and, should the occasion arise, to enlarge it, by force if necessary; to safeguard its fecundity by maintaining and developing the system of irrigation canals on which the crops depended; and to ensure justice, to prevent the strong from oppressing the weak.

Representative of the divine world, in particular of the god of the city who was the real ruler, the king could have a double lineage, at once human and divine. His divine lineage permitted him to share with the gods certain qualities that made him a perfect man in all ways. The king was sometimes endowed with a heroic stature that expressed his superior rank, and his physical strength in addition to his courage rendered him fearless in the hunt and invincible in war. He must be wise, to govern humankind, and pious, to serve the gods. Piety was an essential quality for the proper functioning of the city and the state. The first duty of the king was thus to build and decorate the temples—the residences of the gods—and to see that the rites required for their well-being were duly performed, including libations, sacrifices, festivals, and rituals.

One of the most important rites was that of the sacred marriage, a union of god and goddess that took place every spring in the privacy of the temple to ensure the prosperity of the land throughout the year. Originally it was a marriage between Inanna, the goddess of love, and the shepherd-king Dumuzi, but it could also take place between other divinities. By the time of the Third Dynasty of Ur, and probably even earlier, this rite was actually performed by the king, who thus took the place of the god as one of the marriage partners.

The resemblance between the qualities of the gods and of kings led naturally to the deification of certain rulers. Two kings of Agade—Naram-Sin and Sharkalisharri—and some of those of the Third Dynasty of Ur wrote their names preceded by the determinative sign for *divinity* and adopted for their representations attributes or attitudes borrowed from images of the gods. On his great victory stela now in the Louvre, Naram-Sin wears a headdress decorated with horns like those of the gods (see "The Birth of Writing," fig. 11). The kings of Ur appeared on numerous cylinder seals enthroned like divinities before their worshipers. Sanctuaries were built for these kings, and their statues inside them were maintained like those of the gods. But, as Thorkild Jacobsen has commented, the deified king did not really become a god, and his deification did not denote a division of character between mortal and immortal; rather deification was understood as the expression of royal function.[4]

Chosen by the gods, Gudea enjoyed the particular favors of the three great tutelary divinities of the state, each of whom was the child of one of the three principal gods of the Sumerian religion. Ningirsu, the lord of Girsu, was the son of Enlil, god of the sky and chief of the pantheon. His sister Nanshe, the diviner of the gods, was the daughter of Enki, the god of wisdom and of subterranean waters, and lived in the city of Nina. Gatumdug, daughter of An, the god of the sky, was the mother of Lagash, founder of this city where she resided. The goddess Bau, wife of Ningirsu, was also the daughter of An; their sons were Shulshaga and Igalim.

Gatumdug first chose Gudea for a son, as the prince (whose real parents are unknown to us) himself proclaimed in a prayer to the goddess: "I have no mother, you are my mother; I have no father, you are my father; you gave birth to me in the temple" (Cyl. A, III, 7–8). But Gudea was chiefly "given the scepter by Ningirsu" (Statue D, IV, 5–6), and the entire pantheon of Lagash assembled to enthrone him "the day when Ningirsu chose Gudea for the country, like a good shepherd" (Statue B, III, 6–9). Nanshe looked upon him with a favorable eye; he was guided by Bau's speech; Nindara, the husband of Nanshe, gave him strength; Shulshaga gave him the breath of life; and Igalim offered him the scepter of sovereignty (Statue B, II, 1–19).

In his writings as well in his images, Gudea emphasized his religious role over his political role. The latter was not neglected, but it seemed to be absorbed by the former. We know, for example, by the name he gave to one indicated by the military campaign already mentioned.

In his inscriptions Gudea related indefatigably the many pious building projects he carried out and dedicated essentially, but not exclusively, to the divinities of the city. The building of the Eninnu, the temple of Ningirsu, seems to have been the great project of his reign; two hymns, each written on a large clay cylinder, recount different stages of its construction. The first, known as Cylinder A, describes the building of the sanctuary; the second, Cylinder B, describes the ceremonies accompanying the dedication of the temple (fig. 4). Built according to rites and at Ningirsu's command communicated to Gudea through the intermediary of a dream that the goddess Nanshe interpreted, the sanctuary was furnished, decorated, and filled with gifts offered by the prince and populated with divine servants. It contained the room where the sacred marriage between the god and his wife Bau was to take place, the union on which depended the prosperity of the land. Gudea's piety thus benefited the entire population and became in itself a political act.

The emphasis the prince placed on his religious activities, evident in the texts, can also be seen in the monuments he has left, all dedicated to divinities. Among them, the fragments of stelae recovered primarily from the Eninnu can serve as illustrations to the texts describing the building of this sanctuary. According to a passage in Cylinder A (XXIII, 1–3 through XXIV, 1–3), in seven days Gudea set up seven stelae in different places within the Eninnu and gave them each a name. Near one of the gates of the

Figure 4. Cylinder B of Gudea, Tello (ancient Girsu), southern Iraq, ca. 2120 B.C. Terracotta, 22 × 12¾ in (56.5 × 33 cm). The inscription in Sumerian describes the installation of the deity Ningirsu in his newly constructed temple.

of the years of his reign that he took particular care to maintain and develop the system of irrigation canals. We also know by certain rites accompanying the construction of the temple that he sought to make justice and understanding prevail among his subjects (Statue B, VII; Cyl. A, XII 21–XIII 15). Yet he did not disregard an opportunity to engage in warfare, as

Figure 5. Personal cylinder
seal of Gudea, Tello (ancient
Girsu), southern Iraq, ca.
2120 B.C. Drawing from im-
print on clay, height approx. 1
in (2.7 cm). The seal shows
the prince brought by his personal deity before Ningirsu,
guardian deity of Lagash.

goddess, is led by the hand in front of an enthroned god by his personal god Ningishzida, who is identified by the horned serpents adorning his shoulders and who could himself be preceded by a divine intermediary.

One side of the stela depicts different episodes in the building of the temple, including the transportation of materials across mountainous lands and by river and maritime routes, and the construction itself, carried out by workers carrying baskets of bricks on their heads and climbing on ladders. The other side shows the ceremonies that took place in the completed temple, with the installation of gifts offered by Gudea, a list of which is given in Cylinder B. Depicted on the reliefs are a chariot, a young ass, weapons, a lyre, and sculptures of lions probably intended to guard the gates of the temple. The fragments of the reliefs also show a figure carrying a copper foundation statuette of a kneeling god grasping a peg, similar to actual examples inscribed with the names of Gudea and Ur-Bau (fig. 6). There were also processions of standard-bearers, scenes of libation, and scenes of music with singers, drums, and lyres sometimes decorated with a bull's head (fig. 7). A small fragment preserved in the archaeological museum in Istanbul that shows a file of prisoners is the only allusion to a military victory. It may depict Gudea's campaign against the Elamites, but, as mentioned in the inscription on Statue B (see fig. 12), since the captured booty was offered to Ningirsu, even the representation of this military episode acquired a religious character.

The theme of Gudea's stelae has a

sacred enclosure wall of the temple of Ningirsu, the archaeologist Gaston Cros found fragments that did not constitute a complete monument but that, when combined with other fragments recovered from different places at the site of Tello, give us an idea of the genre of reliefs carved in Gudea's workshops. These were large stelae curved at the top, probably decorated on four sides with scenes carved in relief and arranged in registers; they no doubt resembled the famous stela of Ur-Nammu now in the University Museum in Philadelphia. The themes of decoration are the same—the building of the temple and the ceremonies that took place afterward. These stelae thus illustrate by means of figured decoration all of the long poems inscribed on cylinders A and B.

At the top are depicted scenes of presentation analogous to those which decorate the personal cylinder seal of Gudea (fig. 5). The prince, bareheaded and holding a palm, sometimes followed by a supplicating

Figure 6. Foundation peg dedicated by Ur-Bau, Tello (ancient Girsu), southern Iraq, ca. 2130 B.C. Copper, 11¼ × 3¼ in (29 × 8.5 cm)

Figure 7. Stela depicting musicians, Tello (ancient Girsu), southern Iraq, ca. 2120 B.C. Limestone, 47 × 24¾ in (120.5 × 63.5 cm)

great antiquity. A cult vase from the site of Uruk dating to about 3000 B.C. shows a long procession of figures, arranged in registers, led by the "priest-king" who brings the offerings of the entire city to the temple. Beginning in this period relief sculpture served as official art representing specific activities of the ruler. His political role as warrior and hunter and his religious role were treated equally until the middle of the third millennium. Then the empire of Agade emphasized representations of victory, while the Sumerian renaissance emphasized scenes of cult.

Certain objects offered by Gudea to the gods have come down to us so that we can see actual examples of the vases and basins mentioned in the texts or depicted on the reliefs. There are also maceheads of exceptional size, adorned with carved lions' heads or lacking decoration altogether. The most spectacular of the offerings that survived is the libation vase of the prince, intended for the cult of Ningishzida (fig. 8). Made of steatite (soapstone), it is decorated with acolytes of this chthonic god: two serpents intertwine around a staff whose top joins the mouth of the vase, and a horned dragon with serpent body, reptilian scales, and scorpion tail holds a gatepost symbolizing the entrance of a sanctuary. The raised figures of the serpents and the dragon confront each other. The water of the libations was poured out not only through the mouth of the vase but also through two holes pierced in the mouth of the serpents. The vase is inscribed: "To Ningishzida, his god, Gudea, prince of Lagash, dedicated [this]."

The rite of libation is known to us through numerous representations from the Neo-Sumerian period (fig. 9). The worshiper is usually nude, but if he is the ruler he is dressed and wears a soft hat with a tall brim, known as the royal cap. He pours the water into a large footed vase, from which emerge symbolic plants.

Another kind of votive offering seems to have been peculiar to the princes of the Second Dynasty of Lagash. Gudea, his brother-in-law Ur-Gar, and the wife of his son Ur-Ningirsu dedicated to various divinities statuettes in the form of reclining

Figure 8. Libation vase of Gudea, Tello (ancient Girsu),
southern Iraq, ca. 2120 B.C.
Steatite (soapstone), 9¼ ×
4¼ in (23.6 × 11 cm)

bulls with human heads (fig. 10). On the back of each statuette is a small cavity that probably held a miniature vase intended for modest offerings. These beneficent monsters, prototypes of the later guardian bulls of Assyrian palace gates, appeared in Early Dynastic iconography in scenes of animal combats or as symbols of the mountain, particularly that of the east, from which the sun god appeared.

It was customary for relatives of the rulers or certain of their subjects to dedicate statues or cult objects, inscribed for the life of the prince, and place them in temples. Two statuettes were thus dedicated to goddesses by two wives of Gudea; one of them, Ninalla, was the daughter of Ur-Bau. And the beautiful sculpture known as the Woman with a Scarf, unfortunately fragmentary and now lacking an inscription, certainly represents a princess of his family (fig. 11).

The extraordinary collection of some twenty statues of Gudea, which

were placed in different sanctuaries of Girsu to perpetuate the life of the prince, emphasize the same sentiments of piety. Yet the wish to express the majesty of the ruler can also be perceived. He is seated or standing, hands joined, dressed in a draped robe that leaves the right shoulder bare.[5] Sometimes he is bareheaded, but more frequently he wears the royal cap. His bare feet are sculpted in a niche that assures the solidity of the monument according to a tradition initiated at the end of the Early Dynastic period. Most of his statues bear an inscription naming the divinity to whom the statue was dedicated. The inscription describes in varying length and detail the construction of the temple, its location, and its furnishings. It then describes the making of the statue itself and adds the important fact that the prince gave it a name. This name is in the form of a short phrase that alludes to the favor of the divinity or formulates a wish for the life of Gudea. In some cases

Figure 9. Modern clay impression of cylinder seal of a governor of the city of Nippur, dedicated to the deity of fire for the life of Shulgi, king of Ur, ancient Sumer, southern Iraq, ca. 2094–2047 B.C. White agate, 1¼ × ½ in (3.4 × 1.2 cm). The king makes his libation before the standing deity in the presence of the goddess Lama.

Figure 10. Statuette of a
human-headed bull, ancient
Sumer, southern Iraq, ca.
2120 B.C. Black steatite (soapstone), 4¾ × 5¾ in (12.1 ×
14.9 cm)

the text ends with curses against
whoever removes or breaks the statue
or erases its inscription. In addition,
there is often a cartouche, separated
from the inscription proper, which
gives the name of Gudea, generally
followed by his title and sometimes
accompanied by a brief epithet. Some
inscriptions also refer to other pious
building projects.

Most of the statues come from
Tello (ancient Girsu), where they were
found at the end of the nineteenth
century by the French diplomat and

archaeologist Ernest de Sarzec. Some,
however, reached the antiquities market as a result of clandestine excavations carried out at the site between
authorized excavation campaigns.
Another statue was removed from
Tell Hammam, a site near Tello, by W.
K. Loftus in 1850 and is now in the
British Museum. Although fragmentary, it was the first statue on which
the name of Gudea could be read, at a
time when this prince was still unknown.

The inscribed statues from Tello

Figure 11. Woman with a Scarf, statuette of a princess, Tello (ancient Girsu), southern Iraq, ca. 2120 B.C. Steatite (soapstone), 7 × 4½ in (17.8 × 11.8 cm)

can be divided into two different groups distinguished by size. Eight of them, together with a large fragment, came to the Louvre in 1881 following the first excavations by Sarzec. They decorated the palace of an Aramaean prince constructed in the second century B.C. on the ruins of the ancient temple of Ningirsu that Ur-Bau and Gudea had built some two thousand years earlier. The other group consists of six statues dedicated by Gudea in the nearby temples of his personal god Ningishzida and of Ningishzida's wife Geshtinanna.

The first group is quite homogeneous. The statues are large; one, known as the Colossal Statue, is greater than life-size.[6] They are all made of diorite, and Gudea notes on all but one that the stone was imported by him from the land of Magan. All are also, unfortunately, headless.

The most famous of the group is the one known as the Architect with a Plan, whose long inscription, like that of Cylinder A, describes the construction of the Eninnu (fig. 12). The inscription also mentions the circumstances of the setting up of the statue itself. Given speech by Gudea, it was charged by him to remind the god of his pious actions and to stand in the "place of libations," its gaze fixed on Ningirsu. This "place of libations" was, it seems, the principal court of the temple, perhaps also the place where offerings were made to the dead. The prince depicted himself as the builder of the temple, following a tradition initiated at Lagash around 2475 B.C. by the Sumerian king Ur-Nanshe. Instead of carrying a basket of bricks on his head like his distant predecessor Ur-Nanshe, however, Gudea depicted himself holding on his knees the plan of the temple that was revealed to him by the god (fig. 12a). It was probably the sacred enclosure of the Eninnu, a veritable rampart, of which Cros recovered impressive remains. Cylinder A tells us that the sanctuary of Ningirsu was in fact a holy city consisting of the main temple and numerous annexes and different cult places.

Two other statues of this group

Figure 12. Architect with a Plan, Statue B of Gudea, dedicated to Ningirsu, guardian deity of Lagash, Tello (ancient Girsu), southern Iraq, ca. 2120 B.C. Diorite (greenstone), 36½ × 18 × 24¼ in (93 × 46 × 62 cm)

The last three statues were dedicated to three goddesses: one to Gatumdug, the mother of Lagash, on the occasion of the building of her temple in that city; the two others to Ninhursag, the great Sumerian goddess and mother of Ningirsu (fig. 13), and to Inanna, the goddess of love, in their sanctuaries at Girsu.

In the second group are three small seated statues made of diorite dedicated to Ningishzida and three standing statues dedicated to Geshtinanna.[8] Only one comes from authorized excavations; this is the small statue of Gudea, seated, in the Louvre, whose head was recovered by Sarzec in 1900 and the body by his successor, Cros, in 1903 (fig. 14). The five others appeared on the antiquities market following clandestine digging in 1924. In contrast to those discovered on the ancient site of the Eninnu, these are complete and show the prince wearing the royal cap. They are also smaller in scale.

The seated statues dedicated to Ningishzida differ from those of the first group primarily in scale and in that their inscriptions do not mention the source of the stone. In contrast, the three statues dedicated to Geshtinanna form a distinctly separate series, both because of the stone from which they are carved and because of iconographic peculiarities.

The Gudea from the Stoclet collection, recently acquired by the Detroit Institute of Arts, is made of paragonite.[9] Instead of the right hand's joining the left hand in the usual way, it rests on the closed left hand. This gesture is not unique to the era of Gudea but it is rare, attested only on representations of minor divinities. The costume

were dedicated to Ningirsu and two to his wife Bau.[7] Three of their inscriptions list the wedding presents intended for the goddess, which were brought before her in procession in her temple in the holy city. Statue D, the Colossal Statue, mentions the construction of the boat that was to transport Ningirsu and the gifts. Statue G recounts the ceremony of the delivery of gifts. Details about the gifts are given in the inscription of Statue E.

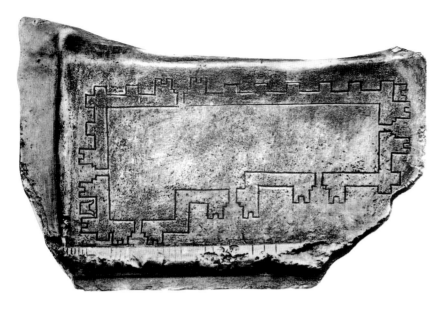

scription that adorns the front of the dress, and fall into four vases sculpted in relief on the base of the statue. Fish that take the form of the waves of the water seem to swim against the current. This vase, a symbol of fertility, is generally a divine attribute. It is most often seen held by Enki, the god of the sweet waters of the deep, or by his acolytes, minor divinities or heroes

Figure 12a. Detail, Architect with a Plan. Length 11¼ in (29 cm)

differs from that of the others by a double line that underscores the neck and shoulder and a trimming of tassels surmounted by a triple fold below. The rings of Gudea's cap are arranged in a quincunx on the brim and in concentric circles on the crown.

The rings of the cap on the Gudea statue in the Ny Carlsberg Glyptothek in Copenhagen[10] and another in the Louvre, made of steatite and calcite respectively, are arranged in concentric circles throughout. These statues are remarkable for their squat proportions. But the most unexpected feature, as frequently observed, is the vase with flowing streams that the Louvre Gudea statue holds (fig. 15). The vase has a globular body, high neck, and wide rim; it is a form already depicted on the cylinder seal of Sharkalisharri, king of Agade. Gudea holds it with both hands; his left hand encircles the body of the vase, his right hand, its neck. Two quadruple streams flow from the neck, descend symmetrically on either side of the in-

Figure 13. Statue A of Gudea, dedicated to the goddess Ninhursag, Tello (ancient Girsu), southern Iraq, ca. 2120 B.C. Diorite (greenstone), 48⅓ × 20½ in (124 × 52.5 cm)

Figure 14. Small statue of seated Gudea, dedicated to his personal deity Ningishzida, Tello (ancient Girsu), southern Iraq, ca. 2120 B.C. Diorite (greenstone), 18 × 9 × 8¾ in (46 × 23 × 22.5 cm)

graphic peculiarity suits the personality of Geshtinanna, which is difficult to pin down. This goddess, whose name means "vine of the heavens," is usually known as the sister of Dumuzi, god of vegetation who dies every year in summer and whom, according to some hymns, she replaces during six months of the year in the netherworld. The cult of Geshtinanna is already attested in the city of Lagash during the Early Dynastic period, in the middle of the third millennium, and Ur-Bau built a temple to her in Girsu; but she does not appear as the wife of Ningishzida until the reign of Gudea. The epithets ascribed to her by Ur-Bau and Gudea could surely clarify her identity during their reigns, but scholars disagree on the interpretation of the terms. One of them, which appears in the inscription of the three standing statues in the second group dedicated to Geshtinanna, has been translated by Bendt Alster as "the queen who lets water and fire grow." [11] Perhaps the vase with flowing streams held by Gudea represents this aspect of the goddess Geshtinanna.

The statue of Gudea's son Ur-Ningirsu (see fig. 3), of which the body is owned by the Louvre and the head by the Metropolitan Museum of Art, is dedicated to Ningishzida. It certainly derives from the same sacred complex consisting of the temples of this god and his wife and in some respects is connected to the series of three statues dedicated to Geshtinanna. It is not made of diorite but of a gypseous alabaster; its scale is modest, measuring 21½ inches (55 cm) in height; and it is distinguished by a base decorated with offering bearers

with nude bodies and curled hair. The vase can, however, also serve as an attribute of other gods. The divinity Gudea approaches on his cylinder seal (see fig. 5) holds two of these vases and is seated on the same motif repeated several times. This figure is probably Ningirsu, god of the storm, dispenser of fertilizing water. But one could also imagine that this icono-

Figure 15. Statue of Gudea holding flowing vase, dedicated to the goddess Geshtin-anna, Tello (ancient Girsu), southern Iraq, ca. 2120 B.C. Calcite, 24¼ × 10 in (62 × 25.6 cm)

or foreign tribute bearers sculpted in low relief. This last feature recalls some of the royal statues of Agade, which rested on bases decorated with representations of the corpses of defeated enemies.

Other statues lacking inscriptions—two in the Louvre and one in the Cleveland Museum of Art—and a series of heads, for the most part wearing the royal cap (see fig. 1), complete the ensemble of works attributed to Gudea. They are unable to help answer questions about the relative dates of the entire group of statues or their precise meaning.

To answer the first question, scholars have studied the formal characteristics of the sculptures and the contents of their inscriptions, but the results have been inconclusive and at times even contradictory. In trying to determine relative dates, scholars examine the proportions of the figure, the realism of the representation, and other characteristics suggesting the age of the individual depicted. The proportions may have been selected to show a more or less slender body (and thus a more or less youthful individual), or they may have been determined by a purely arbitrary canon. Guitty Azarpay, who follows the generally accepted opinion that the proportions of the finished statue depend essentially on the form of the uncarved block of stone, has recently studied the dimensions of several statues of Gudea by means of photogrammetry. She has concluded that the proportions of the large statues made of diorite were conceived as the superposition of six well-defined units corresponding to the length of the forearm, or cubit; the units were re-

duced vertically for the statues of smaller scale. Recent studies also suggest that the smaller statues belong to the beginning and intermediate phases of the reign of Gudea; the larger ones are later and would have been carved at the time when diorite could be imported without difficulty in the form of large blocks.[12]

The youthful aspect of the face of Gudea on the three statues dedicated to Geshtinanna seems to confirm this hypothesis. Yet, if one considers the clear evolution toward a greater realism evident between the statue of Ur-Bau and those of Ur-Ningirsu, one encounters a difficulty. The statue of Ur-Bau, with its short canon and its rigidity, represents a clear regression by comparison with Akkadian royal statues, while the face of a bust of Ur-Ningirsu, now in Berlin, is rendered with great realism.[13] From this perspective, the Stoclet Gudea could, with some difficulty, be placed at the beginning of the reign.

It also is possible that differences in style are due not to a chronological development but to peculiarities of different workshops, with the finest statues destined for the great divinities of Lagash and the more modest ones to the personal god of the ruler and to his wife. One could also wonder whether the princely effigies sought to render particular features of the ruler or to present an image of his royal function. Indeed, several heads show the same wide face with prominent cheekbones, a facial structure very different from those of the small statues from Tello. One could imagine that these were really features of the prince if other statues, such as the Stoclet Gudea or the head in Philadelphia, did not show a more elongated outline.

In any case, there is a clear desire to emphasize the power and majesty of the subject. Different elements converge to convey immediately that one is in the presence of someone out of the ordinary: the scale, the costume, the evoking of particular physical and moral characteristics. The exceptional number and scale of the statues also mark Gudea apart from other humans. The scale of the Gudea statues is particularly striking compared to the small effigies of princesses, such as that of his wife Ninalla (measuring only 6⅝ inches without the head) or the Woman with a Scarf (see fig. 11). The diorite used for statues of the prince, a material that could be imported only by a powerful ruler from distant regions across the sea, reinforces majesty. So does the togalike robe, which is seen for the first time on a bust of the Akkadian king Naram-Sin about 2240 B.C. and continued to be represented on statues of rulers engaged in official ceremonies until the time of Hammurabi (reigned 1792–1750 B.C.). The cap with a tall brim, at Lagash decorated with curls that suggest a kind of fur, was worn thereafter by kings from Ur-Nammu to Hammurabi.

The message conveyed by the physical characteristics of the statues is more subtle but probably more significant. Irene J. Winter has analyzed what she calls the "visual properties" of the statues of Gudea that imply strength not only by their scale but by the proportions of the body and by vigorous musculature. The prominence of the eyes and the seriousness of the expression convey a sense of wisdom and piety.[14] It seems legitimate to think that what was sought was a moral rather than a realistic portrait of Gudea, a portrait that expressed the qualities one expected of a ruler.

The original placement of the seated statues has been much debated. Scenes of presentation of a worshiper to a deity or intermediary depicted on stelae or on cylinder seals always show the worshipers standing in the presence of the divinity. The seated position seems to imply equality among the different seated personages or their superiority in relation to those who stand. Could the statues of seated personages, their hands clasped, represent the faithful in the act of prayer in the temple, or do they have another meaning? The Architect with a Plan (see fig. 12), the image of Gudea as the king who builds, was set up not in the *cella*—the innermost room containing the cult image—but, as explicitly stated in its inscription, in a place called the *ki-a-nag*, interpreted variously by scholars as an open space for libations or a place of cult offering to Gudea himself. This last suggestion seems difficult to accept, since Gudea was not deified until after his death.

The series of statues of Gudea belong in a long tradition of royal images that appeared with the beginnings of monumental sculpture. From the "proto-urban" period are statues of a "priest-king" recognizable by his headband and his rounded beard. In the Early Dynastic period statues of worshipers were made in large numbers, and those of officials are distinguished not by their superior quality but only by their inscription

Figure 16. Statue of Ebih-il, dedicated to the goddess Ishtar, Mari, Syria, ca. 2500 B.C. Alabaster, 20½ × 2¼ × 11¾ in (52.5 × 20.6 × 30 cm)

or sometimes by their hairstyle (fig. 16). Yet one of these, dedicated at Ur to the god Enlil by the prince of Lagash, Enmetena, could be seen as a distant model for those of Gudea.[15] Not only is it made of diorite, a stone rarely used in that period, but it bears a long inscription recalling the pious building projects of the ruler, who gave it the name Enlil Loves Enmetena. The sculpture of the Akkadian empire that has come down to us is almost exclusively royal. It shows the king generally in life-size scale, wearing a skirt or, beginning with Manishtusu, a draped and fringed robe (fig. 17). The sculpture testifies to a new interest in realism. Most examples are made of diorite (actually, gabbro) imported from Magan; some are made of bronze. While the Akkadian king expresses his piety through his attitude of prayer, he also depicts himself equally as a royal warrior by recalling in the inscription his victorious campaigns or showing the bodies of defeated enemies on the base of the statue. From this court art Gudea retained the characteristics expressing majesty and royal power but eliminated any bellicose aspect. Following his reign, the official sculpture of the Third Dynasty of Ur is poorly known. A small statue of the king Shulgi, made of diorite and found at Ur, seems modest compared to those of the prince of Lagash[16]—but then evidence is entirely dependent on the chance of excavations.

Throughout the centuries, the figure of the king can generally be recognized by scale, details of dress, and the pose of conqueror, builder, or offering bearer. Most often the face of the ruler is treated in the same style as those of his subjects, especially in the art of the Neo-Assyrian and Persian periods in the first millennium B.C. It was not by creating a portrait in our sense of the word that the princes of the ancient Near East sought to perpetuate their images. Instead, they intended the image to represent them eternally in front of the gods. What was essential for them was undoubtedly to perpetuate their actions and their names by the power of words preserved in the inscriptions, conveying the majesty of their function through characteristics understandable to everyone. Though the images

Figure 17. Statue of Manishtusu, king of Agade, ca. 2260 B.C. Diorite (greenstone), 34¼ × 21½ in (88 × 55 cm). The statue was brought as war plunder from the city of Agade in Babylonia to Susa, southwestern Iran, in the 12th century B.C.

of Gudea seem at times to record the face of an individual, they were actually intended to preserve an archetype.

## Notes

1. The major texts of Gudea are found on two large cylinders made of baked clay, known as A and B, which describe respectively the construction of the temple of Ningirsu and the setting up of the cult statue of the god in his new home. Other important texts are found on the statues of Gudea, which are distinguished by means of letters (A, B, etc.). A first translation of texts was given by François Thureau-Dangin in *Les inscriptions de Sumer et d'Akkad* (Paris: E. Leroux, 1905), pp. 104–99. Subsequent inscriptions are translated from this source, and citations appear in the text.

2. Piotr Steinkeller, "The Date of Gudea and His Dynasty," *Journal of Cuneiform Studies* 40, no. 1 (1988): 47–53.

3. Quoted in Samuel Noah Kramer, "Kingship in Sumer and Akkad: The Ideal King," *Le palais et la royauté*, ed. Paul Garelli, XIXᵉ Rencontre Assyriologique Internationale, (Paris: Paul Geuthner, 1974), pp. 163–76.

4. Thorkild Jacobsen, "Early Political Development in Mesopotamia," *Zeitschrift für Assyriologie*, n.s. 18 (1957): 138, n. 108.

5. This is a ceremonial costume that ought to have prevented any physical activity and the exact arrangement of which has been difficult to understand. Léon Heuzey saw it as a rectangular piece of cloth fringed on the short sides, rolled around the body so as to leave the right arm and shoulder bare and to cover the left arm and shoulder completely. But the experiments he made on living models produced a multitude of awkward folds and made the lower edge of the skirt uneven. Either the costume of the statues is highly stylized, or it must have been partly sewn or adjusted with pins, as Agnes Spycket has suggested in *La statuaire du Proche-Orient ancien* (Leiden: E. J. Brill, 1981), p. 188. Alternatively, perhaps the costume was made of several pieces of cloth, as Donald Hansen has hypothesized in "A Sculpture of Gudea, Governor of Lagash,"
*Bulletin of the Detroit Institute of Arts* 64, no. 1 (1988): 13. See also Léon Heuzey and Jacques Heuzey, *L'histoire du costume dans l'antiquité classique: L'Orient* (Paris: E. Leroux, 1935), pls. xxx, xxxiii; Eva Strommenger, "Mesopotamische Gewandtypen von den frühsumerischen bis zur Larsazeit," *Acta Praehistorica et Archaeologica* 2 (1971): 46–47.

6. The standing statues G, E, and C are between 1.24 and 1.43 m in height; the seated statues H, F, B, and D are, respectively, 0.77, 0.86, 0.93, and 1.58 m.

7. These are Statue D, called the Colossal Statue, and Statue G, With the Broken Shoulder, dedicated to Ningirsu. Statue E, With Broad Shoulders, and Statue H, also called the Small Seated Statue, were dedicated to Bau.

8. Seated statues: Louvre, height 46 cm (see fig. 14); Metropolitan Museum of Art, height 44 cm; Iraq Museum, Baghdad, height 30 cm (lacking the head, which is in the University Museum, Philadelphia). Standing statues: Louvre, height 62 cm (see fig. 15); Ny Carlsberg Glyptothek, Copenhagen, height 63 cm; Detroit Institute of Arts, height 41 cm.

9. Hansen, "Sculpture of Gudea," (1988): pp. 5–19.

10. Flemming Johansen, *Statues of Gudea, Ancient and Modern*, Mesopotamia 6 (Copenhagen: Akademisk Forlag, 1978), pls. 55–60.

11. Ibid., p. 54.

12. Guitty Azarpay, "A Canon of Proportions in the Art of the Ancient Near East," in *Investigating Artistic Environments in the Ancient Near East*, ed. Ann C. Gunter (Washington, D.C.: Arthur M. Sackler Gallery, 1990), pp. 93–103; Irene J. Winter, "The Body of the Able Ruler: Toward an Understanding of the Statues of Gudea," in DUMU-E₂-DUB-BA-A: *Studies in Honor of Åke W. Sjöberg*, ed. Hermann Behrens, Darlene Loding, and Martha T. Roth, Occasional Publications of the Samuel Noah Kramer Fund 11 (Philadelphia: University Museum, 1989), pp. 573–83.

13. Winfried Orthmann, ed., *Der Alte Orient* (Berlin: Propyläen Verlag, 1975), fig. 64.

14. Winter, "Body of the Able Ruler," pp. 573–83.

15. Orthmann, *Der Alte Orient,* fig. 31.

16. *Ibid.,* fig. 63.

## Further Reading

Falkenstein, Adam. *Die Inschriften Gudeas von Lagash*. Analecta Orientalia 30. Rome: Pontificium Institutum Biblicum, 1966.

Magisterial study of the historical, religious, and literary contexts of the reign of Gudea.

Frankfort, Henri. *The Art and Architecture of the Ancient Orient*. 4th ed. New York: Penguin Books, 1977.

The classic textbook for ancient Near Eastern art and architecture, first published in 1954; notes and bibliography have been revised and updated.

"Gudea." In *Reallexikon der Assyriologie*, vol. 3, no. 9 (Berlin: Walter de Gruyter, 1972). Part A: "Nach Texten," by Adam Falkenstein, cols. 676–79; part B: "Archäologisch," by Eva Strommenger, cols. 680–87.

Reference articles covering textual and art historical sources, which also provide extensive scholarly bibliographies.

Hansen, Donald P. "A Sculpture of Gudea, Governor of Lagash." *Bulletin of the Detroit Institute of Arts* 64, no. 1 (1988): 5–19.

A study of the statue of Gudea formerly in the Stoclet collection, now in the Detroit Institute of Arts.

Johansen, Flemming. *Statues of Gudea, Ancient and Modern*. Mesopotamia 6. Copenhagen: Akademisk Forlag, 1978.

Exhaustive study of the statues of Gudea, tending to show that the majority of the statues of Gudea acquired on the antiquities market are fakes. In an appendix, "In Defense of the Authenticity of a Statue of Gudea," Bendt Alster studies the inscription of the Stoclet Gudea (now in the Detroit Institute of Arts) and shows that it must be authentic.

Orthmann, Winfried, ed. *Der Alte Orient*. Berlin: Propyläen Verlag, 1975.

A compendium of articles on the art and architecture of the ancient Near East, written by a variety of scholars and richly illustrated.

Parrot, André. *Tello: Vingt campagnes de fouilles (1877–1933)*. Paris: Albin Michel, 1948.

A very useful synthesis on the discoveries at Tello, written by one of the excavators of the site.

Sarzec, Ernest de, and Heuzey, Léon. *Découvertes en Chaldée*. Paris: E. Leroux, 1884–1912.

A collection of reports published as the excavations proceeded over a period of nearly thirty years. Sarzec wrote the account of the excavations, Heuzey that of the objects, and Arthur Amiaud and François Thureau-Dangin that of the inscriptions. A publication of interest for the history of the discoveries and also for its wealth of beautiful illustrations.

Spycket, Agnes. *La statuaire du Proche-Orient ancient*. Leiden: E. J. Brill, 1981.

A detailed, well-illustrated survey of statuary in the ancient Near East.

Strommenger, Eva. "Das Menschenbild in der alt-mesopotamischen Rundplastik von Mesilim bis Hammurapi." *Baghdader Mitteilungen* 1 (1960): 1–103.

This scholarly monograph discusses the statues of Gudea as part of a larger study of statues of human figures from early Mesopotamia.

Winter, Irene J. "The Body of the Able Ruler: Toward an Understanding of the Statues of Gudea." In DUMU-E₂-DUB-BA-A: *Studies in Honor of Åke W. Sjöberg,* ed. Hermann Behrens, Darlene Loding, and Martha T. Roth, pp. 573–83. Occasional Publications of the Samuel Noah Kramer Fund 11. Philadelphia: University Museum, 1989, pp. 573–583.

---

Note: Louvre accession numbers: Figure (1) AO 13; (2) AO 9; (3) AO 9504; (4) MNB 1511; (5) AO 3541; (6) AO 311; (7) AO 52; (8) AO 190; (9) AO 22312; (10) AO 2752; (11) AO 295; (12) AO 2; (13) AO 8; (14) AO 3293; (15) AO 22126; (16) AO 17551; (17) Sb 47

# The Epics of Gilgamesh

*Maureen Kovacs*

Two thousand years of Mesopotamian civilization produced a vast literature of epics, myths, philosophy, fables, proverbs, and poetry, in addition to courtly, cultic, scholarly, and technical texts. Among these the epic of Gilgamesh holds a special place for both the humanist and the scholar. Unlike most Mesopotamian literature, concerned with social, political, cosmological-theological, and cultic matters, the central themes of the epic of Gilgamesh are personal and transcend cultural boundaries—loneliness, love, loss, fear, and rage at human fate. These are developed within a story of exotic adventures, producing a work of emotional depth and narrative drama that engages the modern reader even across the chasm of three thousand years. It is only since the decipherment of cuneiform in the 1850s that the epic has been known to the modern world, and only much more recently that good English translations have allowed this extraordinary piece of literature to be appreciated beyond the circle of specialists. The epic deserves attention not only as an early example of the process of mythmaking but for its in-

dependent value as a fine work of literary creativity (see Selected Passages from the Epic of Gilgamesh).

## The Historical Gilgamesh

It appears that oral traditions about famous kings were written down almost as soon as cuneiform script could express the language. The historical Gilgamesh[1] ruled in the southern Mesopotamian city of Uruk, probably toward the end of the Early Dynastic II period (ca. 2700–2500 B.C.). Although no contemporary inscriptions of him have been discovered, a few have been found that prove the existence of persons he is associated with in literature, including an archaic fragment telling about Lugalbanda, his father, which is believed to date from about 2500 B.C. At present, the earliest mention of Gilgamesh is in late Early Dynastic II tablets listing gods of all Sumer, among them the deified kings Lugalbanda and Gilgamesh. A votive vessel bears a dedicatory inscription to the deified Gilgamesh, and offerings were also made in various cities to him.

Figure 1. Tablet of the standard version of the epic of Gilgamesh, Nineveh, Iraq, Neo-Assyrian period, ca. 800–600 B.C. Clay, 5¼ × 5¾ × 1¼ in. (13.3 × 15 × 3 cm). British Museum. The tablet containing the text of the Flood story from Tablet XI is restored from many fragments.

# Selected Passages from the Epic of Gilgamesh

## Gilgamesh

Supreme over other kings, lordly in appearance,
he is the hero, born of Uruk, the goring wild bull.
He walks out in front, the leader,
and walks at the rear, trusted by his companions.
Mighty net, protector of his people,
raging flood-wave who destroys even walls of stone!
Offspring of Lugalbanda, Gilgamesh is strong to
    perfection,
son of the august cow, Rimat-Ninsun, . . . Gilga-
    mesh is awesome to perfection.
It was he who opened the mountain passes,
who dug wells on the flank of the mountain.
It was he who crossed the ocean, the vast seas, to
    the rising sun,
who explored the world regions, seeking life.
It was he who reached by his own sheer strength
    Utanapishtim, the Faraway,
who restored the sanctuaries (or: cities) that the
    Flood had destroyed . . . for teeming mankind.
Who can compare with him in kingliness?
Who can say like Gilgamesh: "I am King!"?
Whose name, from the day of his birth, was
    called "Gilgamesh"?
Two-thirds of him is god, one-third of him is human.
(I, 28–46)

## The Cedar Forest

They stood at the forest's edge,
gazing at the top of the Cedar Tree,
gazing at the entrance to the forest.
Where Humbaba would walk there was a trail,
the roads led straight on, the path was excellent.
Then they saw the Cedar Mountain, the Dwelling
    of the Gods, the throne dais of Irnini.
Across the face of the mountain the Cedar
    brought forth luxurious foliage,
its shade was good, extremely pleasant.
. . . . . . . . . . . . . . . . . . . . . . . . . . . . . . . . . . . . . . . .

## The Capture of Humbaba

The ground split open with the heels of their feet,
as they whirled around in circles Mt. Hermon
    and Lebanon split.

The white clouds darkened,
death rained down on them like fog.
Shamash raised up against Humbaba mighty
    tempests—Southwind, Northwind, Eastwind,
    Westwind, Whistling Wind,
Piercing Wind, Blizzard, Bad Wind, Wind of
    Simurru,
Demon Wind, Ice Wind, Storm, Sandstorm—
    thirteen winds rose up against him and covered
    Humbaba's face.
He could not butt through the front, and could
    not scramble out the back,
so that Gilgamesh's weapons were in reach of
    Humbaba. (V, 1–8, 123–33)

## The Monument to "My Friend"

Just as day began to dawn, Gilgamesh . . .
and issued a call to the land:
    "You, blacksmith! You, lapidary! You, copper-
        smith!
    You, goldsmith! You, jeweler!
    Create 'My Friend,' *fashion a statue of him.*
    . . . he fashioned a statue of his friend.
    His Features . . .
    . . . , your chest will be of lapis lazuli, your
        skin will be of gold." . . .
    "I had you recline on the great couch,
    indeed, on the couch of honor I let you recline,
    I had you sit in the position of ease, the seat at
        the left, so the princes of the world kissed
        your feet.
    I had the people of Uruk mourn and moan for
        you,
    I filled happy people with woe over you,
    and after you (died) I let a filthy mat of hair
        grow over my body,
    and donned the skin of a lion and roamed the
        wilderness." (VIII, 53–60, 81–87)

From: Maureen Gallery Kovacs, *The Epic of Gilga-mesh* (Stanford, Calif.: Stanford University Press, 1989), pp. 4, 41, 43–44, 71.

"Gilgamesh" is occasionally used as a theophoric element in personal names.

For other information we have to rely on later, nonarchival sources, such as the Sumerian King List, the hymns and epics composed about 2100 B.C., and other products of the royal court environment. The statements are often contradictory, as "history" in ancient Mesopotamia was written to serve the present and therefore subject to revision as needed. The royal hymnic tradition names Gilgamesh as the son of Lugalbanda and the goddess Ninsun and as the "brother and friend" of Ur-Nammu and Shulgi, two founding kings of the dynasty at Ur, a neighbor city to Uruk (see The Sumerian Texts about Gilgamesh). Ur-Nammu transferred the cult of Lugalbanda and Ninsun from his native city, a part of Uruk, to Ur. The motivation was political, for these upstart kings of Ur strove to rule all Sumer and needed to legitimate their rule by claiming to be the true heirs of Uruk. Uruk, under the (alleged) historical Gilgamesh, had successfully challenged the supremacy of the established dynasty (see the epic "Gilgamesh and Agga" in The Sumerian Texts about Gilgamesh), and Uruk had also freed Sumer from foreign rule. Ur-Nammu's funerary hymn refers to Gilgamesh's revealing the judgments from the netherworld, and in later Mesopotamian religion Gilgamesh's chief function is as judge or administrator of the netherworld. Even Gudea, governor of Lagash (ca. 2120 B.C.), claimed that he was raised together with Gilgamesh, but the import of this connection is not clear.

The Sumerian King List is a fascinating but problematic document in Mesopotamian history. It states that the father of Gilgamesh was a "lillu-spirit" (meaning unknown) and separates Gilgamesh from Lugalbanda "the Shepherd" by another king. It also names a son of Gilgamesh who succeeded him to the throne; another historiographic text states that the father and son embellished a major sanctuary in Nippur. The son is, however, conspicuously absent in the Sumerian and Akkadian epics. The King List identifies Gilgamesh's grandfather Enmerkar as the builder of Uruk, and in hymns it is specifically said that Enmerkar built the wall of Uruk. The earliest claim that the wall was built by Gilgamesh comes from a votive inscription of about 1800 B.C. from a king of Uruk who restored the city wall, "the ancient work of Gilgamesh."

Given the unclear, conflicting, and tendentious nature of the early sources, the "real," historical Gilgamesh is only a pale shadow of his brilliant legend.[2] His friend Enkidu, who figures prominently in the epics, is unknown outside of the epic tradition except perhaps for one curious reference in an Old Babylonian incantation in which Enkidu is he "who established the watches of the night as three."[3]

## The Writing of the Gilgamesh Legends

In truth, there is not a single "epic" of Gilgamesh but several distinct "epics" about Gilgamesh (see The Development of the Gilgamesh Traditions).

The earliest were written in the Sumerian language, about 2100 B.C. in Ur, and consist of six separate epics, myths, and hymns that do not constitute a single composition (see The Sumerian Texts about Gilgamesh). Although composed for propaganda purposes by the first two kings of the Third Dynasty of Ur, the texts contin-

ued to be copied for several hundred years in the scribal schools. By about 1800 B.C. some of the Sumerian material was adapted by a creative scribe, writing in the Akkadian language, to form the core episode of a much longer and intellectually sophisticated epic of Gilgamesh whose main theme was the fear of death and the search

## The Sumerian Texts about Gilgamesh

The six Sumerian-language compositions—"epics," myths, and hymns—about Gilgamesh are believed to have been composed around 2100 B.C. by the court scribes of the first kings of the Third Dynasty seated in Ur, Ur-Nammu and Shulgi. In royal hymns these kings claimed the gods and former kings of the neighboring city of Uruk as their ancestors; they are "brother and friend" of Gilgamesh and "son" of the goddess Ninsun and the deified Lugalbanda, Gilgamesh's parents. There was strong political motivation for these claims, and these first Sumerian tales composed about Gilgamesh do not simply record ancient oral traditions for their own sake but consciously shape "history" to serve the interests of their sponsors.

The Sumerian tale "Gilgamesh and the Cedar Forest" provides the raw material for the core of the Old Babylonian epic. While walking along the wall of Uruk, young Gilgamesh sees a body floating down the river and becomes aware of human mortality, especially his own. He determines to do something grand before the oblivion of death, to make fame live forever after him. He persuades his servant, Enkidu, to undertake a dangerous journey to the Cedar Forest (in the east, Iran) to set up a stela or monument in his name. Weapons are prepared, and the two set off, accompanied by a group of citizens. After crossing seven mountains they reach the forest, and Gilgamesh cuts down a tree. The divinely appointed guardian of the Cedar Forest, Huwawa* is outraged and puts on protective auras that stun Gilgamesh into terrible visions. Gilgamesh relates the ominous visions to Enkidu, who nonetheless urges him on. Gilgamesh disarms Huwawa by verbal trickery and shackles him. Then Gilgamesh has a magnanimous change of heart and would free him, but Enkidu protests vehemently and kills Huwawa himself. When Enkidu later presents the head of Huwawa to the chief god Enlil, the god is furious and curses both men for killing the guardian. Enlil then distributes the auras of Huwawa to nature. The fear of death, the leitmotif of the later Akkadian epics, is already present in this Sumerian tale.

Another text, "Gilgamesh in the Netherworld" or "The Death of Gilgamesh," is a death lament for Gilgamesh. It contains the central theme of the second half of the Akkadian epic—the search for eternal life: Enlil, the father of the gods, "has destined thy fate, O Gilgamesh, for kingship, for eternal life he has not destined it." Later, "He lay on the bed of destined fate, unable to get up."** The text possibly accounts for how Gilgamesh came to be the "lord" or "judge" of the netherworld, in compensation for not being granted eternal life. This text resembles the hymn to the deceased King Ur-Nammu, Shulgi's predecessor, suggesting that it might have been recited during ceremonies for deceased ancestors, recent and ancient.

"Gilgamesh and the Bull of Heaven" is clearly the prototype for part of Gilgamesh's encounter with Ishtar and the bull of heaven in the standard version, Tablet VI. Only part of the middle of the tablet remains. Here the goddess refuses to allow Gilgamesh to administer justice in her sanctuary, probably causing him to turn against her. She demands the bull of heaven from her father, the god Anu. He first refuses, but he gives in when she threatens to cry out to the other gods. The actual killing of the bull by Gilgamesh and Enkidu and the conclusion are not preserved.

The curious myth "Gilgamesh, Enkidu, and the Netherworld" is nearly complete but seems to have been used only marginally in the integrated Akkadian epic. The introduction sets the time after the cosmos had been ordered. Enki, god of the subterranean waters, journeys over a raging sea to the netherworld. A certain tree for immortality. Less than half of this Old Babylonian–period epic, which probably consisted of five to seven tablets, is preserved, so understanding of the entire narrative still eludes us. What we do have is stylistically fresh and lively and evidences a coherence that makes it essentially an original creation. The standard version of the epic represents the final stage of revision of the Old Babylonian original and is the text commonly referred to and translated as the epic of Gilgamesh. While the basic themes and story line remain the same, important changes in emphasis, style, and content mark the standard version as a distinct composition. Though this

growing on the bank of the Euphrates had been uprooted by the wind. The goddess Inanna replants it in her garden in Uruk, waiting to make a chair and bed of its wood. However, a serpent, a demonic bird, and a demoness take over the tree. Inanna asks the sun god to help, but he ignores her. She then turns to valiant Gilgamesh, her "brother," who drives the invaders away, gives her the wood, and makes a stick and a ring (or perhaps it is a ball) from the base. With these sporting implements he oppresses the men of Uruk, perhaps by constant athletic competitions. When the widows and girls complain, the implements fall down into the netherworld, and Gilgamesh's servant Enkidu volunteers to bring them back. This task can be done only by stealth, as a man cannot leave the realm of the dead. Enkidu disobeys all Gilgamesh's advice on how not to be noticed, and he is seized by the netherworld. Gilgamesh protests to two gods that since Enkidu did not really die—not by disease, accident, or war—he therefore was improperly seized by the netherworld. Finally the god Enki instructs the sun god to open a hole in the ground, from which the ghost of Enkidu briefly emerges. The implements that occasioned the journey to the underworld are forgotten, and Enkidu reports on the conditions of those below. The wormy decay of the body horrifies Gilgamesh. Those who fare well are those with many sons and family, the innocent stillborn, and those who experienced sudden unexplained deaths. The barren and those dying before marriage or without family or in accidents fare miserably. The tablet ends, but without the usual statement of the end of a composition; perhaps the fate of Enkidu is contained in some other concluding fragment.

The appearance of Gilgamesh in this myth may be quite secondary. Only a little of the second half of the myth seems to have been used in the Akkadian eleven-tablet epic. The motif of the oppression of the men of Uruk is used in the epic to prompt the creation of Enkidu, who then puts an end to Gilgamesh's aggressive competitions. Enkidu's observations of the netherworld are paralleled by his dream of the netherworld, but the content is not the same. Gilgamesh's horror at bodily decay is a constant refrain in the second half of the epic. On the other hand, the entire section concerning Gilgamesh, Enkidu, and the netherworld is translated verbatim and appended as Tablet XII, an artificial and inconsistent addition by a late editor.

Another fragment appears to deal with the burial of Enkidu, the subject of Tablet VIII of the standard version.

A last, short epic of historical-political reference, "Gilgamesh and Agga," does not seem to have been used in composing the Old Babylonian epic. King Agga of Kish in northern Mesopotamia sends his envoys to enforce his sovereignty over Uruk. The city elders would give in, but the young men agree to resist. Enkidu prepares the troops and makes a "terrifying aura." Agga is ultimately captured through tricky word play and the aura, but Gilgamesh remembers that once in the past Agga had spared him, so he releases the now-humbled Agga.

* The Cedar Forest was located in or beyond Elam in southwestern Iran. The name of the guardian, Huwawa/Humbaba, derives from the name of the chief god of the Elamite pantheon, Humpan. In the Akkadian-language versions the Cedar Forest was relocated to northwest Syria, the new source of timber.

** S. N. Kramer, trans., in *Ancient Near Eastern Texts Relating to the Old Testament*, ed. James B. Pritchard, 3d ed. (Princeton, N.J.: Princeton University Press, 1969), p. 50, l. 35.

version was produced in southern Mesopotamia in several stages between 1600 and 1200 B.C., virtually the only tablets from this period come from outside—from Anatolia, Syria, and Canaan—and show many local non-Mesopotamian adaptations. The main extant sources for the standard version are tablets from 800–200 B.C. The epic consists of eleven tablets and contains approximately three thousand lines, about 60 percent of which are preserved. The fragments belong to some eight to twelve copies of the epic found in royal, temple, and possibly private libraries in Babylonia and Assyria (fig. 1). The eleven-tablet epic is framed by a repeated opening and concluding passage and is formally complete. At some time in the late second millennium B.C. a scribe added a twelfth tablet, probably because it related to Gilgamesh's role as judge of the netherworld, which was still important in funerary rituals. The twelfth tablet is generally considered to be an "inorganic appendage," inconsistent with the preceding tablets in content and style. The following summary is based on the standard version, with missing passages sometimes restored from the Old Babylonian version for the sake of narrative continuity, even though the Old Babylonian is quite different in style and often in content.

## Summary of the Epic

The first tablet opens with a narrator praising the wisdom of Gilgamesh, a famous king of old who left eternal monuments of both his royal and personal accomplishments. According to the narrator, the epic of Gilgamesh was written by Gilgamesh himself, and the very tablet (or stela) on which he wrote his experiences was deposited in the foundation of the city wall of Uruk, where it remains for all to read.

Gilgamesh is described as two-thirds divine and one-third human, extraordinary in strength and beauty. Yet he oppresses the young men and women of his city Uruk in some way, and the gods react by creating a counterpart to him. In sharp contrast to Gilgamesh, Enkidu is a primal man, not born of human parents but raised in the wilderness with the wild beasts, whom he sets free from traps. These super- and subhuman counterparts are brought together in a classic confrontation of civilization and nature, as a trapper employs a harlot from Uruk to engage Enkidu in prolonged sex, so depleting his strength. Abandoned by the wild, Enkidu now feels the need for emotional intimacy: "Becoming aware of himself, he sought a friend."[4] The harlot tells him of the beautiful but oppressive Gilgamesh. In an outburst of righteous indignation, Enkidu resolves to best Gilgamesh in a contest of strength, though the harlot reminds him that the gods have favored Gilgamesh from birth.

Meanwhile Gilgamesh has strange dreams that his mother, the goddess Ninsun, interprets to mean that he will meet a mighty companion whom he will love "like a wife." After Enkidu has been taught the ways of civilized men, even working as a night watchman chasing away the wild animals, his former comrades, the harlot takes him to meet Gilgamesh in Uruk. They arrive during a festival, and

# The Development of the Gilgamesh Traditions

• Ca. 2600 B.C.: The historical King Gilgamesh of Uruk. There are no contemporary texts, but oral traditions are assumed.

• Ca. 2500 B.C.: Gilgamesh, as deified ancestor, is mentioned in temple tablets among the many gods who receive offerings. The earliest extant epics about his father Lugalbanda also date from this period.

• Ca. 2100 B.C.: Six separate Sumerian-language compositions about Gilgamesh were produced under the patronage of the kings of the Third Dynasty of Ur, especially King Shulgi. Two are political-historical; two are mythical; and the others concern death and burial and belong to the realm of the funerary cult. Extant tablets date to 1800–1600 B.C. Only one text ("Gilgamesh, Enkidu, and the Netherworld") is maintained in the literary tradition after that time.

• Ca. 1800–1600 B.C.: The Old Babylonian period epic, composed in the Akkadian language probably by one author, is a single long narrative drawing on and integrating the plots and themes of most of the Sumerian texts as well as much other unrelated literature. Probably five to seven tablets long, only some 40 percent or less remains. Everything after the killing of Humbaba is lost except Gilgamesh's meeting with the tavern keeper and the ferryman. The seven or eight extant tablet fragments are from several sites in Mesopotamia, suggesting that variant editions may have already been circulating.

• Ca. 1600–1100 B.C.: In the Middle Babylonian period only one fragment is extant from Mesopotamia itself. However, the Old and Middle Babylonian versions must have been known outside of Mesopotamia as Akkadian was used as the international language of diplomacy (ca. 1400–1300 B.C.), and cuneiform script and literature were taught in Anatolia, the Levant, and Egypt. Fragments were discovered at Emar in Syria and Megiddo in Canaan. In the Hittite kingdom of central Anatolia an Akkadian-language version of probably three tablets covers the events at least up to Enkidu's death. The text generally resembles the later standard version, but it also shows connections to the Old Babylonian; this is an intermediate, provincial version. Also from the Hittite kingdom are meager fragments of adaptations of the Gilgamesh epic and possibly the Humbaba epic in the Hurrian language, and Hittite-language versions—probably derived from the Hurrian, not the Akkadian—stress the adventures in the Cedar Forest, which are of local interest. A small fragment written in alphabetic Ugaritic cuneiform seems to contain a few words reminiscent of the Cedar Forest episode and may possibly be a Ugaritic-language translation or version. The Old Babylonian epic (in one or more versions) underwent a long process of revision by mid- and late-second millennium author-editors, evolving toward the end of this period into a relatively standardized text with eleven tablets. The Mesopotamians of the first millennium B.C. themselves attributed "authorship" of the epic to a priest of Uruk named Sinleqqiunninni, who probably lived in the thirteenth century B.C. The standardization of the text by this time is inferred from the fact that first-millennium texts from both Assyrian and Babylonian sites are very similar, indicating a common source.

• 1000–200 B.C. The standardized text that took shape in the Middle Babylonian period is attested in fragments of the first millennium, coming from both northern and southern Mesopotamia. This standard version, as modern scholars designate it, is what is commonly meant by "the" epic of Gilgamesh, the only version complete enough for translation. The extant fragments belong to some eight to twelve copies of the epic found in royal, temple, and possibly private libraries in Babylonia (Uruk, Babylon) and Assyria (Nineveh, Nimrud, Assur, Sultantepe). The eleven-tablet epic contains approximately three thousand lines, of which about 60 percent are preserved. Their content and wording are fairly consistent, but the late tablets from the city Uruk may reflect a slightly different edition.

For details on chronology of the epics, see Jeffrey H. Tigay, *The Evolution of the Gilgamesh Epic* (Philadelphia: University of Pennsylvania Press, 1982).

Figure 2. Clay masks of Humbaba, Ur, southern Iraq, Old Babylonian period, ca. 2000–1600 B.C. Average height 4 in. (10¼ cm). University Museum, University of Pennsylvania

when Enkidu learns that Gilgamesh engages in certain sexual behavior with women (not yet understood), he blocks Gilgamesh's passage out of jealousy, or perhaps misguided moral outrage. They wrestle, and for the first time Gilgamesh recognizes he has met his match, just as foretold in the dreams. He breaks off the contest to avoid defeating Enkidu, who then acknowledges Gilgamesh as the legitimate, divinely appointed superior.

The two become devoted friends, the first time either has felt true companionship. Gilgamesh's mother laments Enkidu's lack of "breeding" in compassion, or possibly disgust: "Enkidu has no father or mother, his shaggy hair no one cuts. He was born in the wilderness, no one raised him" (II, 157–59). Overhearing this, Enkidu breaks down sobbing in grief and

loses all strength and spirit. A long and probably important passage is missing here.

Gilgamesh then proposes a dangerous adventure to the Cedar Forest. There he and Enkidu will slay the guardian, Humbaba the Terrible (fig. 2), cut down the sacred cedar, and achieve eternal fame. Enkidu knows firsthand Humbaba's divinely ordained powers, and he protests. So do the citizen advisers, but despite their warnings and the tearful pleadings of his mother, Gilgamesh and Enkidu set off under the promised protection of the sun god.

During the six-day journey Gilgamesh has terrifying and ominous dreams, but Enkidu interprets them favorably, so they go on. At the primeval Cedar Forest, however, Enkidu wants to turn back, realizing the gravity of their trespass. The sun god urges them on, and they soon confront Humbaba the Terrible.

The interchanges with Humbaba are, unfortunately, fragmentary and difficult to understand; Humbaba shows naked hostility to his old animus Enkidu ("who does not even know his own father," v, 78) and tries to make a bargain with the respected King Gilgamesh ("your mother gave birth to you," v, 135). Eventually Enkidu persuades Gilgamesh to kill Humbaba (figs. 3, 5), but not before Humbaba hurls a final curse portending Enkidu's early death. Gilgamesh and Enkidu cut down cedars, and Enkidu cuts down the highest one to make a door for the temple of the chief god and thus to placate him for

their killing of the guardian and cutting of the trees.

Back in Uruk, the hero Gilgamesh is approached by the goddess Ishtar, who wants him to marry her. Knowing the fates of her other loves, he rejects her violently and incurs her enmity. She sends the bull of heaven down to desolate the land, but the two friends manage with matadorlike skill to slay it (fig. 4).

Faced with the friends' double offenses of killing the guardian of the Cedar Forest and the bull of heaven, the gods decide that Enkidu must die, despite the sun god's admission of responsibility. In despair at this fate and injustice, Enkidu lashes out bitterly at the cedar door and at the trapper and harlot who introduced him to human

Figure 3. Modern clay impression of a cylinder seal showing the slaying of Humbaba, Neo-Assyrian period, ca. 800–600 B.C. Amber chalcedony seal, height 1¼ in. (3.14 cm). Collections of Dr. Leonard Gorelick

Figure 4. Modern clay impression of a cylinder seal possibly showing the killing of the bull of heaven, Neo-Babylonian period, 612–539 B.C. Blue chalcedony seal, height 1 in. (2.8 cm). British Museum

life. Reminded that this was also the means for his friendship with Gilgamesh and told that he will be magnificently memorialized, Enkidu recants and blesses the harlot.

Beginning to sicken, Enkidu has a nightmare that he is about to be seized by a demon and Gilgamesh does not even try to save him. Enkidu dreams he is taken down into the netherworld, "the House of Darkness . . . where those who enter do not come out" (VII, 176), where dwell the pathetic remains of the once-famous. But just as it seems his fate is to be read out from the Tablet of Destinies,

the tablet of the epic breaks off. When the text resumes Enkidu asks only that Gilgamesh "remember me and forget not all that I went through [with you]" (VII, 249). At the end of his long illness Enkidu rallies and with his last, delirious words accuses Gilgamesh, faithfully watching by his deathbed, of having abandoned him.

Gilgamesh is devastated by Enkidu's death and refuses to accept its reality: "Now what is this sleep that has seized you?!" (VIII, 43). He does not allow his friend to be buried "until a maggot fell out of his nose" (X, 136). Then, in profound mourning,

Gilgamesh performs elaborate funerary rituals and has a rich statue called "My Friend" built in Enkidu's memory. Formerly death was to Gilgamesh a distant abstraction, to be overcome by achieving fame. Now confronted with personal loss and the horror of bodily decay, he comes to fear his own death. He abandons civilization, reverting to the wild state of nature in which Enkidu used to live, but finds no solace. He then determines to seek out the secret of eternal life from the only man known to have attained it, the survivor of the Flood, Utanapishtim.

A strange, troubling dream marks the beginning of Gilgamesh's quest, the text of which is very poorly preserved. At the pass to the road of the sun, through the netherworld at night, the keepers warn him of the impossibility of his venture but allow him to go on. He emerges at dawn into a fabulous jeweled garden bordering the sea. There a wise tavern keeper (a "beer-maid") also tries to dissuade him from his futile pursuit but finally directs him to the ferryman of Utanapishtim, who will take him across the sea. In a rage of desperate impulsiveness, Gilgamesh destroys parts of the boat, but they nevertheless manage to make the crossing with punting poles and a makeshift sail.

Finally meeting the legendary Flood hero, Gilgamesh repeats, for a third time, his saga of sorrow and pleads for surcease. Utanapishtim's response is a long soliloquy on life and death, which is unfortunately one of the most obscure, garbled, and unsatisfying passages in the whole epic. Utanapishtim then recites a version of the Flood story, borrowed from another Mesopotamian myth.[5] He was spared because of his obedience to his personal god and given eternal life at the remote Mouth of the Rivers. Clearly this was a one-time exception made under extraordinary circumstances. Utanapishtim nevertheless puts Gilgamesh to a test of his potential for immortality by challenging him to go without sleep. Gilgamesh fails utterly and feels death closing in all around him: "In my bedroom Death dwells, and wherever I set foot there, too, is Death!" (XI, 239–40).

Utanapishtim's wife urges her husband to give Gilgamesh a consolation gift so he does not have to return to his city broken and empty-handed. The Flood hero then reveals the existence of a "plant of rejuvenation" that will restore Gilgamesh's now-ravaged youth and enable him to live his life over again with the benefit of his new knowledge. Gilgamesh, weighted by stones like a pearl diver, plucks the plant from the bottom of the sea. He saves the plant, intending to test it on an old man of Uruk before trying it himself. The hesitation is fatal, for Gilgamesh loses the plant to a passing serpent: "At that point Gilgamesh sat down, weeping, his tears streaming over the side of his nose" (XI, 299–300). After all he had been through, the only thing he had to show for it ended up to the benefit of a snake, which is rejuvenated by sloughing its skin.

Gilgamesh returns home older and empty-handed after all, for there are no second chances in real life. The story of his quest ends where it began, echoing the words of Tablet I that marvel at the extraordinary wall encompassing Uruk. Gilgamesh has learned, finally, to accept the limitations of his humanity. The wall, which will outlast him, is symbol of the only immortality available to humanity: noble accomplishment. But implicit in praise of the wall is praise for the epic itself, which Gilgamesh wrote down and enclosed within it for the benefit of future generations.

## The Literary Creativity of the Epic

The epic of Gilgamesh just described is a carefully crafted literary composition whose unifying motif is the journey—both external adventure and personal journey to self-understanding. Stylistically the epic is formal and often prolix, consciously building expectation and peaks of emotional intensity. It incorporates allusions to numerous other literary compositions and is clearly the product of an intellectual-academic steeped in the literary traditions of Mesopotamia. In ancient Mesopotamia, scribes were trained by copying existing texts, but they also created literary compositions and edited earlier ones. While the proficiency of the Gilgamesh author-editor accounts for the epic's richness of meaning, it appears, too, that he sometimes misunderstood his source and sacrificed content for form. The result stands in marked contrast to the original Old Babylonian version, which, in the few passages that we can compare, is far more lively, vivid, and coherent but much less sophisticated. A few examples will illustrate the nature of some of the changes between the original and the standard version.

In the original, Gilgamesh dreams of an ax and what might be a meteorite, portending his confrontation and his friendship with Enkidu. The later version imposes an artificial parallelism on the dreams, combining elements of both and generally confusing the two (I, 226–73). The standard version also adds a philosophical meaning to what is a simple human reaction in the original. After Enkidu's six days and seven nights with the harlot, the original states: "He forgot the wilderness where he was born"[6] and then Enkidu agrees to be taken to Uruk. In the standard version the act of intercourse signals domestic man's alienation from nature and, at the same time, the dawning of feeling, attachment, and self-awareness:

> The gazelles saw Enkidu and darted off,
> the wild animals distanced themselves from his body.
> Enkidu . . . his utterly depleted(?) body,
> his knees that wanted to go off with his animals went rigid;
> But then he drew himself up, for his understanding had broadened.
> Turning around, he sat down at the harlot's feet,
> gazing into her face, his ears attentive as the harlot spoke. . . .
> What she kept saying found favor with him.
> Becoming aware of himself, he sought a friend. (I, 179–95)

At some point, about 1500 B.C., an entire episode was added that was not in the original. Tablet VI, the feisty confrontation of Gilgamesh and Ishtar and the dramatic killing of the bull of heaven, is not at all essential to the development of the story. Based on the Sumerian myth "Gilgamesh and the Bull of Heaven" (see The Sumerian Texts about Gilgamesh), it was incorporated into the epic by what we might call an "encyclopedist" editor, who must have felt compelled to integrate *all* known Gilgamesh traditions. The formal tie-in with the following Tablet VII is awkward and betrays its secondary nature.

Surely the most significant difference between the two versions lies in Gilgamesh's encounter with the tavern keeper (Tablet X). In the original it seems likely that Gilgamesh sought out eternal life, or knowledge of eternal life, from her. She fails him, offering only practical, almost grandmotherly, or possibly hedonistic, advice to stop fighting the inevitable and to enjoy his life:

> The life that you are seeking all
>   around you will not find.
> When the gods created mankind
> they fixed Death for mankind,
> and held back Life in their own
>   hands.
> Now you, Gilgamesh, let your belly
>   be full!
> Be happy day and night,
> of each day make a party,
> dance in circles day and night!
> Let your clothes be sparkling clean,
> let your head be clean, wash your-
>   self with water!
> Attend to the little one who holds
>   onto your hand,
> let a wife delight in your embrace.
> This is the (true) task of *man-
>   kind*(?)[7]

Gilgamesh is astounded and deeply insulted: "What are you saying, tavern-keeper? . . . My heart is grieving for my friend, . . . My heart is grieving for Enkidu!"[8] How dare she imagine his love and grief for Enkidu—his second self—could be consoled by ordinary family life. Clearly she has not appreciated the extraordinary, and possibly homoerotic, nature of their relationship. If this is the best human wisdom can offer, Gilgamesh must seek further, across the sea, for Utanapishtim, the survivor of the Flood.

In the standard version this entire dialogue is intentionally omitted, perhaps because at the beginning of his journey in the wilderness (Tablet IX) Gilgamesh has already determined to seek out Utanapishtim, who knows the secret of eternal life. He therefore does not seek enlightenment from the tavern keeper but asks only for directions. Indeed in the standard version the meeting with the tavern keeper becomes no more than a stepping-stone to Utanapishtim and an opportunity for the author-editor to build emotional intensity through an impassioned twenty-seven-line-long monologue by Gilgamesh on his suffering. The same peroration is repeated at his meeting with the ferryman and yet again with Utanapishtim.

Such examples testify to Mesopotamian literary creativity of the second millennium B.C., when scribe-scholar-authors used existing written material and motifs but recast and reformulated them freely, as their own imaginations and forms of self-expression dictated. By the first millennium B.C. the spirit of innovation in traditional cuneiform literature gradually disappeared. The text of the famous myths and epics of old became fixed, objects of preservation rather than vehicles of a vital, living culture.

## The Afterlife of the Epic

Although knowledge of the epic of Gilgamesh was essentially lost with the end of cuneiform writing, resonances in other ancient literatures and in art attest that the story was known beyond the boundaries of cuneiform

Figure 5. Stone relief showing the "slaying of Humbaba" in a local style, Tell Halaf, Syria, ca. 1000 B.C. Basalt, height 24¼ in. (62.2 cm). Walters Art Gallery

culture (see Illustrations of the Epic of Gilgamesh). First, in the mid-second millennium B.C., when Akkadian was the international language of diplomacy, the epic was known in Akkadian in the Hittite capital of Anatolia, in northern Syria, and at Megiddo in Canaan. It was probably also part of the scribal curriculum at Amarna in Egypt, but so far no fragments of the epic have been found there. In the same period the epic was also adapted and translated into other languages: in Anatolia into Hurrian, and from Hurrian into the Hittite language, and in Syria possibly even into the Ugaritic language.[9]

Some scholars find parallels in the *Iliad* and *Odyssey* to scenes, characters, or episodes from the epic of Gilgamesh. If the resemblances are due to borrowing, the epic probably became known to the Greeks during the mid-second millennium B.C., when connections between the Near East and the Aegean were active. Yet the influence may be at a broad conceptual level, and so the path of transmission difficult to document. A passage in the Latin poet Ovid's *Ars Amatoria*, for example, recounts a primitive man's awakening through intercourse with a woman to the sense of human dignity. In theme it provides a striking

## Illustrations of the Epic of Gilgamesh

Representations of scenes from the epic of Gilgamesh are remarkably few, though this could be largely due to the disappearance of wall paintings and the recycling of metal and stone objects. King Shulgi (ca. 2100 B.C.), in one of his hymns, mentions a statue of Gilgamesh that he installed in a temple in Ur, but this has surely long since disappeared and cannot be expected from future excavations at Ur. Several clay plaques dating to the Old Babylonian period show the killing of Humbaba and may be remnants of a series of illustrations of this episode; their original context is unknown. The vigor and drama of these scenes match the flavor of the Old Babylonian version and stand in contrast to the highly formal and controlled quality of the later version and its artistic representations. Out of the entire repertoire of Mesopotamian glyptic art of the second and first millennia B.C. there are only about eight cylinder seals and two ring stones showing this scene (see fig. 3) and a few decorated metal vessels and an ivory plaque. The scene is found on two metal vessels from Iran and stone reliefs from Anatolia and Syria (see fig. 5), but, as Wilfred G. Lambert explains, it "might have been transferred to myths or legends of those areas so that the original association with Gilgamesh was lost."* The killing of the bull of heaven (fig. 4) appears on just four or five seals from Mesopotamia and one from Iran. Humbaba alone, not in relation to the epic of Gilgamesh, is well known in the visual arts. Large fearsome, grimacing heads were used as architectural elements at the entrance to a temple, evidence of his protective and apotropaic function as known in the epic. Clay masks, plaques, and amulets served similar functions (see fig. 2), while Humbaba's grotesque features were contorted to resemble convoluted entrails for use in divination. Texts relating to first-millennium funerary rituals refer to statues and figurines of Gilgamesh in his capacity as lord of the netherworld, but none has yet been found.

* Wilfred G. Lambert, "Gilgamesh in Literature and Art: The Second and First Millennia," *Monsters and Demons in the Ancient and Medieval Worlds,* ed. Ann E. Farkas, et al., (Mainz: Philipp von Zabern, 1987), pp. 47–48. This article includes a full discussion with illustrations. Lambert does not include BM 89435 among the representations of the epic of Gilgamesh for reasons given on pp. 50–51, 43. Dominique Collon includes BM 89435 as no. 858 in *First Impressions: Cylinder Seals in the Ancient Near East* (Chicago: University of Chicago Press, 1987). See pp. 178–81 for a discussion of several myths, epics, and legends represented on seals.

likeness to the humanizing influence of the harlot on Enkidu, and the scholar William L. Moran has postulated, "It is hard to believe that the anti-primitivism of classical sources does not derive, ultimately, through a long and complicated process of transmission, its general inspiration and even some of its specific lore from Near Eastern sources." [10]

It should be recalled, however, that even when the epic could have been known by another culture, that culture may not necessarily have chosen to borrow or preserve it. The Hebrew Bible contains allusions to persons or stories that were derived ultimately from Mesopotamian sources, most obviously the Flood story, but Gilgamesh is not among them. It has even been proposed that the episode of the plant of rejuvenation and the snake is reflected in "The Tale of Buluqiya" in the *Arabian Nights*.

Finally, two names that could be Aramaic forms of Gilgamesh and Humbaba appear in the first century A.D. Aramaic Book of Giants, part of the Book of Enoch found among the Dead Sea scrolls. The context is extremely fragmentary, but these once dramatic figures were remembered here only as "giants." A much later translation of the Book of Giants into Middle Persian also preserves a name supposed to be Humbaba.

It seems very likely that the epic and other late Mesopotamian literature did not die out altogether in Mesopotamia proper. The evidence is sparse, but hopeful. Recent research in Aramaic and Syriac literature shows that the popular genre of disputation texts derives ultimately from cuneiform prototypes. One Syriac text of the sixth to ninth century A.D. lists the kings after the Flood and some contemporaneous biblical figures; surely it derives from a Babylonian king list. The names are badly garbled, but one could be Enmerkar, Gilgamesh's grandfather, and "Ganmagos" could be Gilgamesh.

With nearly two thousand years of preserved textual history, the epic of Gilgamesh provides a wealth of insights into the nature of literary creativity and literary tradition in ancient Mesopotamia. The author of the original epic in the Old Babylonian period created his fresh version by adapting various earlier stories about a famous king of old, Gilgamesh, and integrating them freely with other traditions and his own imagination, style, and purpose. Because of the skill of the author in transforming this material into a new, coherent whole, there is little suggestion in Old Babylonian of its complex source materials. Several hundred years later, a scholar-author of a more philosophical and didactic mind expanded and revised the Old Babylonian epic into the standard version we know now, with its intense emotions and desperate existential quest. After this period of literary creativity passed, the epic was copied in the Assyrian and Babylonian libraries with only minor changes for many centuries until the demise of cuneiform. With the continual discovery of cuneiform tablets in every season of excavation, it is certain that we will one day have a complete text of the standard epic and perhaps, too, of the original, allowing for a full appreciation of the work of their authors.

## Notes

1. The original Sumerian name was Bilga-mesh. The change to initial *G* occurred in the Old Babylonian period and is now the conventional form of the name.

2. Gilgamesh was not the only ancient king to be honored by hymns and epics; his predecessors were also celebrated in a cycle of epics dealing with relations with Iran. Translations of these extremely difficult and long epics are still not available, but a discussion of them will soon be. Bendt Alster, "The Enmerkar-Lugalbanda Cycle," in *Civilizations of the Ancient Near East,* ed. J. M. Sasson et al. (New York: Scribner's, forthcoming).

3. Walter Farber, *Schlaf Kindchen, Schlaf!: Mesopotamische Baby-Beschwörungen und - Rituale* (Winona Lake, Ind.: Eisenbrauns, 1989), pp. 37–38, 155. The full passage (lines 15–26) is difficult, and the name Enkidu may not be the original reading.

4. Maureen Gallery Kovacs, *The Epic of Gilgamesh* (Stanford, Calif.: Stanford University Press, 1989), I, 195. This summary and all quotations are from this translation. Subsequent references to tablet and line number appear in the text.

5. The Myth of Atrahasis, most recently translated by Stephanie Dalley, *Myths from Mesopotamia* (Oxford: Oxford University Press, 1989), pp. 1–38.

6. *Ibid.,* p. 137. Dalley uses the term "open country" instead of wilderness.

7. See Kovacs, *Epic of Gilgamesh,* p. 85, n. 1.

8. See the Old Babylonian version, x, iii, 18–20, in Dalley, *Myths from Mesopotamia,* p. 150.

9. A small fragment written in syllabic cuneiform seems to contain the words "he will cut off," "cedars." See the tentative edition by John Huehnergard, *Ugaritic Vocabulary in Syllabic Transcription,* Harvard Semitic Studies 326, 1987), pp. 11–12. The connection with the epic was proposed by D. O. Edzard, "Keilschrift," in *Reallexikon der Assyriologie und vorderasiatischen Archäologie,* ed. D. O. Edzard (Berlin: Walter de Gruyter, 1976–80), 5:545a.

10. William L. Moran, "Ovid's *blanda voluptas* and the Humanization of Enkidu," *Journal of Near Eastern Studies* 50 (1991): 122. See also p. 121, n. 4, for a bibliography of possible Mesopotamian material in Greek literature.

## Further Reading

Collon, Dominique. *First Impressions: Cylinder Seals in the Ancient Near East.* Chicago: University of Chicago Press, 1987.

Surveys the history of seal motifs and styles; includes a chapter on scenes from myths, epics, and legends.

Dalley, Stephanie. *Myths from Mesopotamia.* Oxford: Oxford University Press, 1989.

Translations of major Akkadian-language myths and epics, including the standard and Old Babylonian versions of the epic of Gilgamesh.

Kovacs, Maureen Gallery, *The Epic of Gilgamesh.* Stanford, Calif.: Stanford University Press, 1989.

Translation of the Akkadian eleven-tablet epic, with an introduction, glossary, and appendices on Tablet XII and on Mesopotamian languages and writing.

Lambert, Wilfred G. "Gilgamesh in Literature and Art: The Second and First Millennia." In *Monsters and Demons in the Ancient and Medieval Worlds,* ed. Ann E. Farkas et al., pp. 37–52. Mainz: Philipp von Zabern, 1987.

Discusses the relationship of the Sumerian epics to later versions, with a helpful diagram, and shows the two dozen illustrations of scenes from the epic known in art.

Sasson, J. M., et al., eds. *Civilizations of the Ancient Near East.* 3 vols. New York: Scribner's, forthcoming.

Covers the cultures from the Iranian plateau to North Africa during the period from 3000 to 500 B.C., in 170 original essays.

Tigay, Jeffrey H. *The Evolution of the Gilgamesh Epic.* Philadelphia: University of Pennsylvania Press, 1982.

Technical discussion of the differences among various versions of the epic, with citations to the original tablets and a full bibliography.

Maureen Kovacs received her doctorate in Mesopotamian languages and history from Yale University in 1975 and later worked on the Assyrian Dictionary Project at the Oriental Institute of the University of Chicago. She recently translated the epic of Gilgamesh, published in 1989 by Stanford University Press, for college and general use.

# Chronology

| PERIODS | DYNASTIES | | |
|---|---|---|---|
| | Kish | Lagash | Uruk |
| Uruk IV 3300–3100 B.C. | | | |
| Jemdet Nasr 3100–2900 B.C. | | | |
| Early Dynastic I 2900–2700 B.C. | | | |
| Early Dynastic II 2700–2500 B.C. | Mesalim ca. 2550 B.C. | | Gilgamesh ca. 2600 B.C. |
| Early Dynastic III 2500–2350 B.C. | | Ur-Nanshe ca. 2475 B.C. | |
| | | Eanatum ca. 2450 B.C. | |
| | | Enmetena ca. 2425 B.C. | |
| Akkadian 2350–2190 B.C. | AKKADIAN DYNASTY Sargon 2334–2279 B.C. | | |
| | Rimush 2278–2270 B.C. | | |
| | Manishtusu 2269–2255 B.C. | | |
| | Naram-Sin 2254–2218 B.C. | | |
| | Sharkalisharri 2217–2193 B.C. | | |

| PERIODS | DYNASTIES |
|---|---|

Neo-Sumerian
2190–2000 B.C.

SECOND DYNASTY
OF LAGASH

Ur-Bau
ca. 2130 B.C.

Gudea
ca. 2120 B.C.

Ur-Ningirsu
ca. 2110 B.C.

THIRD DYNASTY
OF UR

Ur-Nammu
2112–2095 B.C.

Shulgi
2094–2047 B.C.

Amar-Sin
2046–2038 B.C.

Shu-Sin
2037–2029 B.C.

Ibbi-Sin
2028–2004 B.C.

## Coming in Spring 1992   *The Sense of Place in Japan*

A cautionary tale about the historic post-town of Unno in the Japan Alps is augmented with drawings of its street of inns. Articles on illustrated nineteenth-century guidebooks and "Hiroshige and His Pictures of the Famous Places" also offer insight into the Japanese sense of place.

## Back Issues

To order back copies of *Asian Art*, check off the desired issue(s) and indicate quantity. Themes are indicated. Mail to: Journals Department, Oxford University Press, 2001 Evans Rd., Cary, N.C. 27513. U.S.: individuals $9.95; institutions $20.00; outside U.S.: individuals $12.95; institutions $23.00. For air-expedited delivery to foreign countries, add $5. Smithsonian Associates receive a 20 percent discount.

\_\_\_\_\_ Vol. I, No. 1 Fall/Winter 1987–1988
*Inaugural Issue: Chinese Art*

\_\_\_\_\_ Vol. I, No. 2 Spring 1988
*The Art of Eating and Drinking in Ancient Iran*

\_\_\_\_\_ Vol. I, No. 3 Summer 1988
*Art of India*

\_\_\_\_\_ Vol. I, No. 4 Fall 1988
*Pictures for the Islamic Book: Persian and Indian Paintings in the Vever Collection*

\_\_\_\_\_ Vol. II, No. 1 Winter 1989
*A Lyric Impulse in Japan*

\_\_\_\_\_ Vol. II, No. 2 Spring 1989
*Timur and Fifteenth-Century Iran*

\_\_\_\_\_ Vol. II, No. 3 Summer 1989
*Buddhist Art of South Asia*

\_\_\_\_\_ Vol. II, No. 4 Fall 1989
*Raghubir Singh's Photographs; Mughal Gardens*

\_\_\_\_\_ Vol. III, No. 1 Winter 1990
*Japanese Ceramics, Crafts*

\_\_\_\_\_ Vol. III, No. 2 Spring 1990
*Ancient Chinese Music and Bronzes; Contemporary Chinese Folk Art*

\_\_\_\_\_ Vol. III, No. 3 Summer 1990
*Yokohama Prints*

\_\_\_\_\_ Vol. III, No. 4 Fall 1990
*The Dream Journey in China*

\_\_\_\_\_ Vol. IV, No. 1 Winter 1991
*Games and Asian Art*

\_\_\_\_\_ Vol. IV, No. 2 Spring 1991
*Indonesian Performing Arts*

\_\_\_\_\_ Vol. IV, No. 3 Summer 1991
*East Asian Furniture*

\_\_\_\_\_ Vol. IV, No. 4 Fall 1991
*Art Collecting*

\_\_\_\_\_ Check enclosed, payable to Oxford University Press

Please charge to my \_\_\_\_\_ MasterCard \_\_\_\_\_ VISA

Acct. No. _____  Exp. Date _____

Signature _____
(Credit card order not valid without signature.)

Name_____

Address _____

City/State/Zip _____

Smithsonian Associate Membership no. _____